TIMES OF REFRESHING

TIMES OF REFRESHING

10,000 MILES OF MIRACLE—
THROUGH CANADA

BY

J. EDWIN ORR

" Times of refreshing shall come from the
presence of the Lord." ACTS, 3. 19

WIPF & STOCK · Eugene, Oregon

Wipf and Stock Publishers
199 W 8th Ave, Suite 3
Eugene, OR 97401

Times of Refreshing
10,000 Miles of Miracle—Through Canada
By Orr, J. Edwin
ISBN 13: 978-1-5326-1740-9
Publication date 1/27/2017
Previously published by Zondervan, 1936

CONTENTS

"Either you're a terrible fool about it all, or else it's going to be *ten thousand Miles of Miracle*, Edwin."

—from *CAN GOD——?*

TIMES OF REFRESHING

CHAPTER I

WESTWARD AT SUNDOWN

A LOW sound of moaning fell upon my ears. Woman or child? I wondered which. I heard it again. It seemed to be the last word in misery—the highest pitch of anguish—the deepest note of despair.

I listened sympathetically. Then I heard a child crying; and again the moaning: and then a man's voice.

"Poor things," I thought, "I would not like to be you."

Again the heart-breaking moaning.

"What if I should have to go through it myself?"

I shuddered at the thought. But as the suggestion grew in my mind, all my will power resisted it with the unexpressed words, "Never, *Never !*"

As it was, nearly everyone was seasick. After watching one and another of the passengers glide away from a half-completed meal, and seeing the number at each sitting gradually reduced to a fraction of the original company, I had thought that it was time to "take myself off" as a precaution. So I had two whole days in my cabin: and all the while the good ship *Newfoundland* rolled and tossed and pitched on the wild waves of the stormy North Atlantic. I spent the time sleeping, reading, eating, praying, thinking—chiefly thinking.

.   .   .   .   .

My thoughts ran in cycles—beginning in a strange way, and ending in a way equally unexpected. That day's date was *September* 28, and September 28 has always been an important day in my life—a day of beginnings and endings. Take 1933, for instance. On that self-same date, I commenced to tour the British Isles—without prospects, money, friends, or anything save a shaky faith in the Providence of God. Then take 1934. On the same date I completed the tour—ten thousand miles of miracle in Britain, with a heart full of thanksgiving to God. And between that date and its successor in 1935, what? A much wider field of service opened in Europe, preaching the Word in England, Ireland, Scotland, Wales, Norway, Denmark, Sweden, Finland, Soviet Russia, Estonia, Latvia, Lithuania, Poland, Germany, Holland, Belgium, France, Switzerland, Austria, Hungary, Yugoslavia, Bulgaria, Rumania, Turkey, Greece, Palestine, Italy, Spain, Portugal.

And now what lies ahead? The 28th September, 1935, begins a world tour, a circumnavigation of the globe. I will not be surprised if it ends a year hence. To God all things are possible.

Already the signs of His approval have been in evidence. A friend, whose name counts for much in both the shipping and the Christian worlds, very kindly offered me a passage on one of his ships going west. I accepted. At the last moment I received a

telegram to state that the ship's sailing would be delayed
by about a week—just enough to upset my programme.
So I replied, saying that I would have to decline the
kind offer; and booked a passage in the usual way,
perhaps a little disappointed to see an offer of £20's
value suddenly disappear. But the Lord Who provides
gave me a surprise—on the two succeeding days there
arrived two cheques, each £10. From Liverpool, I
sailed westward at sundown.

.   .   .   .   .

The other day we passed the Giant's Causeway,
and the Giant's Chimneypots, the huge basaltic pillars
which crown the summit of the steep headland.

It brought back the memory of happy holidays a
short time before spent with boyish freedom by Jack
and myself among the glens of Antrim—the beauty
of the coast road—Portrush and this world-famed
spot, but, as we went westward, memory took me
back to the Portsmouth campaign. I had just received
a report from Miss M. Key, the organiser:

"It was only six weeks before that we heard that
Mr. Edwin Orr could visit Portsmouth—it was
holiday time, too. We asked several clergymen and
ministers to come to our house to talk over what
arrangements could be made. Only four came, the
majority being on holiday. So it seemed hopeless,
but for the fact that we had our four Mission Halls,
each seating 150-250 people.

We called our workers together, and placed Mr.
Orr's proposed visit before them with its great
opportunities and its great difficulties. We decided
to ask him to come to each hall in turn, so as to

spread the revival message as much as possible. Best
of all, we started united prayer meetings, and these
increased in numbers and power, God's presence
being wonderfully felt. And the meetings were well
advertised.

On the Saturday evening of his visit, Mr. Orr
spoke in our Copnor Hall, which was packed. It
was full again on Sunday afternoon, and in the evening
—crowded to overflow. On Monday evening many
Christians received definite blessing in the crowded
Winchester Hall.

We then moved to the London Road Baptist
Church at the kind invitation of Rev. John Edmonds.
Although it holds up to 1,500 it was well filled. On
Wednesday, Mr. Orr spoke on 'The Holy Spirit'
to a rapt congregation. He showed from Holy
Scriptures the coming of the Holy Spirit at Pentecost,
His ministry, and the need of every believer to be
filled. At this meeting also, many entered into a new
experience and the presence of the Lord was
manifested.

"On the Thursday evening, his farewell, Mr. Orr
gave an evangelistic address, the church being
crowded as before. The message concerned 'the
suffering Messiah and the atonement for sin.' There
was great power, many saying afterwards that they
had never heard such an address, or such an appeal
to the unsaved. The meeting was quiet but tense
as he brought Calvary before his hearers. At the end,
he appealed for definite decisions. There were many
young people present, and all over the building came
responses to the appeal.

"We thank God for His servant's visit, which will
remain fresh in the memory of many hundreds. It
has been a time of searching and a time of refreshing
such as few of us have ever known before. Unity of

heart was evident, there being present each evening local clergy and ministers and leaders of Christian work, as well as friends from the countryside around. We feel that it is but the beginning of revival. At the foot of every advertisement we put 'Can God send revival to Portsmouth?' We believe He can."

Mr. Ian Thomas carried on the mission and had much blessing, I hear. There were conversions under his ministry at Copnor. Indeed, we had all much to thank God for—I myself received blessing from His hand. I think that the secret of success was its birth in prayer, its continuance in prayer, and our reliance upon God for the power to do what was obviously a necessity— the deliverance of a challenge to lukewarm Christians.

.   .   .   .

Many other memories came crowding into my mind. Chief of these were amusing times in the car. During the six weeks between the Keswick Convention and the departure of the ship from Liverpool, Jack Sherriff and I travelled about 3,000 miles in Great Britain, he—the expert driver and mechanic, I—the learner, but all the time cognisant of the fact that a loving Father's hand was over us protecting us in the hour of possible danger and directing us by a right pathway.

On one journey of 800 miles, I was interested in finding out the cost of running the car, telling Jack that if it cost less than a penny per mile, I would be more than satisfied that it was economical to run compared with any other means. So we kept an accurate note of the mileage, petrol and oil. The total mileage was 800, and we paid exactly *nothing* for petrol and oil, all of which was wonderfully supplied. If the reader is a mathematician, he can prove the claim that it *did* cost less than a penny a mile.

On yet another occasion we were motoring in Monmouthshire. I was driving the car at about 35–40 miles per hour, along twisted, hilly roads. Suddenly, without warning, a herd of bullocks burst out into the road. I braked immediately, and somehow managed to steer between two of the beasts, but a third animal came forward blocking the way. Him we smote in the ribs, and strangely enough, did the car more damage than the bullock. The humorous side of the incident struck both Jack and myself—we had never seen such a look of pained surprise on any human face, never mind a bullock's! The cattle drover agreed that the accident was unavoidable, we repaired the damage, and so ended one of the many funny happenings of "two men in a car."

.   .   .   .   .

After two days of stormy weather, I got up. I was told once by Miss Wakefield MacGill of London of the tactics employed by a mutual friend of ours in his personal work on board ship. He, like myself, found that the little Gospels and Testaments issued by the Pocket Testament League (of which Miss MacGill is the indefatigable secretary) were the best material for use in personal contacts. Our friend, however, commenced talking to people as soon as he got on board so as to get his work done before any passengers became seasick. I found that the seasick ones were even more approachable.

On board the s.s. *Newfoundland,* was a young Anglican clergyman from Nova Scotia, Rector of an Evangelical parish. With him I had many friendly talks, finding him a man of the best type. At seven a.m. on Sunday morning, we had a Church of England Communion service—a very happy one, too, despite the fact that it was so stormy that it was almost impossible to keep the Bread and Wine upon the table. In the evening, we conducted a service together.

Most passengers were confined to cabin, for the wind howled in fury the whole of the voyage. The waves were mountainous, sending sheets of salty spray across the decks. But, as the recurring entry in the diary of Christopher Columbus told its tale, "we sailed on."

CHAPTER II

NEWFOUNDLAND'S TROUBLES

"LAND—I see land! Look—there!"

We looked up at the boy's shout, and there was a general rush to the side of the ship. There it was— a grey bank, on the horizon, which was scarcely discernible. After a brief scrutiny of the line of the horizon, I returned to the game of shuttleboard on the deck.

The last day of the voyage proved to be much more enjoyable than its predecessors. The wind died down, the sun shone brightly, and the ship's rolling became more bearable to the seasick passengers. The captain —a breezy, good-natured man—laughingly asked where all the stowaways had come from, meaning of course that some passengers were showing their faces for the first time. And indeed everyone was glad to see the last of the bad weather.

After five o'clock, we began to see the coast quite clearly—it was beautiful but forbidding. An hour later we took the pilot aboard and made our way through the narrow entrance to the land-locked harbour of St. John's. Dinner over, we made our way ashore.

The problem which weighed upon my mind as I walked up Water Street was a very simple one. Three days were at my disposal in the city—only three days. Was it possible to meet leaders of every walk and discuss and obtain what I wanted to know about Newfoundland? The human answer was an emphatic "No!" The prayer of faith, seeing the necessity and the golden opportunity and ignoring the difficulties, answered "Yes!"

St. John's is a hilly place, and so in the deepening darkness I made my way up, down, and along the streets. It *was* a problem. At last I came across a building bearing the sign, "United Church Gospel Mission." Neither the people living around nor the nearest policeman seemed able to give me any useful information. I liked the flavour of the place, but had to go on without tracing the superintendent. What was I to do? Again, reason said, "It is impossible—give it up. You do not need to hunt around the place. Take it easy." But I really wanted to find someone from whom I could learn details of the spiritual state of the country, and thus be able to pray and to get others to pray for revival in an intelligent way. So I persisted. After half an hour's search I came across the hoped-for connecting link. Inquiring at a house near a church, I found two little boys who volunteered to take me to the minister's house.

It was interesting to listen to the conversation of the little fellows as we walked along the street.

"Yes," said one, "you missed the riots, you know."

"Is that so?"

"Yes, an' it was terrible, too. I stayed indoors—but the others were a-fighting, an' splitting their heads something dreadful."

"And what were they fighting about?" I inquired innocently.

"Well, it was the police and the men that were fighting—you see, Jimmie's father here is an unemployed and he was fighting, an' he got hurt, too, didn't he, Jimmie?"

"Yes," replied Jimmie proudly.

Reports of grave abuses had angered the masses, causing trouble and consequent interference of the police. A Royal Commission had been sent out from Britain, the result of which was the setting aside of the usual government in favour of a Governing Commission entrusted with a mandate for setting the country on its feet and correcting the abuses.

"And the fighting has stopped," said the older boy, "so the men and police have stopped hurting each other, because when the fighting stops there is no good going on with splitting heads. 'Snat right, Jimmie?"

By the time Jimmie delivered his judgment on the matter, we had arrived at the house. I gave them something as a tip, and went up to the house. I was received cordially. My new friend was a man who believed in evangelism, so we got down to discussion. Not content with giving me so much helpful information, he suggested convening a meeting of all the Free Church ministers to carry on the discussion about revival besides having fellowship. So quite contentedly, I enjoyed the motor run back to the ship, calling to see the interior of a couple of churches en route.

Next morning, feeling the need of exercise, I determined to do some climbing. St. John's is built at the end of a land-locked bay, which is shaped like the imprint of a fist in a mould—the wrist being the exit to the ocean. Standing at the entrance, like an ever-watchful lion couchant, is Signal Hill, surmounted by a fort, and behind the hill is a rugged crag of equal height, from which one may obtain a good view of the city, bay, and surrounding country. Choosing the steepest side I decided to scale it.

Now, that morning in the *Daily News* I had noticed the following:—

"Whirling across trans-Atlantic shipping lanes to-night, apparently without finding victims, the tropical hurricane from the Caribbean is reported heading directly for the Grand Banks where the fishing fleets of Canada, Newfoundland, France and Spain take the harvest from the sea. Ships have been forewarned of the storm as it moves north-eastwards after a toll of fifty-four lives and 5,000,000 dollars on the southern islands."

At the bottom there was a strong breeze, but not enough to make the climb dangerous. Quickly scaling the several hundred feet, I reached the top—immediately receiving the impression that the hurricane had arrived at the same time. I was blown flat, finding it difficult to rise. I do not think that I have ever experienced such strength of wind as blew with that particular gust. I was able to balance myself at an angle of sixty degrees to the horizontal—a thing deemed impossible. And when I descended, friends said, "But there was no wind like that down here." No wonder the press described it as a "freak" storm.

During the afternoon I went sight-seeing in my friend's car. At five o'clock came the "Round Table" conference with the ministers, which I much enjoyed. They told me that there were no meetings in any of the churches that night, and regretted that I could not stay to preach on Sunday, or arrange for a prolonged stay.

Later on in the evening, I walked through the streets in search of some sort of week-night service. I found a Salvation Army Citadel, and to my delight at the prospect of fellowship, there was a meeting for soldiers. The Captain announced that there would be a time for testimonies (here a chorus of Amens and Hallelujahs, to which the drummer added a thump on the big drum) after which Brother So-and-So from Somewhere-or-Other would lead the singing (again the chorus and the thump on the drum) and then, as there was a stranger from London in their midst, the latter would deliver a message from the Word (another chorus and two thumps on the drum). I like Army meetings, so I felt heart-warmed.

At least two of the men who testified, had been terrible drunkards, and they told of the change in their lives, how they gave up this, and how they saw that the Lord did not approve of that, and how they got something better instead (here another thump on the drum from the drummer). We had a happy meeting, followed by supper in the Captain's house which was not far away. And so to bed, grateful that the Lord had answered prayer in enabling me to give His message at short notice.

Only one prayer request remained unanswered, one that I might meet the superintendent of the mission hall which I had discovered on the first night on shore. I forgot about it, so after an interesting interview with a clergyman who had risen high in the Anglican Church's service, I got ready to leave for Halifax.

While waiting for the ship to leave, I began to while away the time in a game of dominoes—at the request of the Anglican Rector on board. I was much amused a moment later when we were interrupted so that I might be informed that a gentleman was enquiring for the "Reverend Mr. Orr." I was glad of the interruption, for it enabled me to meet another leader in St. John's. He greeted me with the words:

"I have come to see my daughter off to Boston, and as I saw a nice report of your visit in this morning's paper, I came here looking for you. Could we have a chat?"

This brother added further information from his own angle, and then I discovered that he was the superintendent whom I had sought to meet.

And so ended my very brief visit to Newfoundland. My object was to gain an impression which I might pass on to those of my readers who seek information for their prayers. To them I now give an opportunity to fight a battle for the Lord in Newfoundland—the weapon being intelligent prayer for a mighty revival.

To gain a proper impression of the needs of a country, it is necessary to study other than spiritual facts. In

St. John's, I noticed the following on a commemorative tablet:—

> "*Close to this commanding and historic spot, Sir Humphrey Gilbert landed on the 5th day of August, 1583, and in taking possession of this New Found Land in the name of his sovereign Queen Elizabeth, thereby founded Britain's overseas empire.*"

The history of Newfoundland before that date is mostly guess-work. The island was inhabited by a tribe of Indians who have died out in spite of efforts to preserve the race. It is almost certain that Northmen from the Christian colony of Greenland knew the country as "Vinland," but the actual discovery to civilisation took place when John Cabot reached the island. Since then the country has been settled by British settlers from the three realms.

Although bigger than England, Newfoundland has a population of less than 300,000—considerably less than that of Islington, one of the scores of Metropolitan boroughs in London. The land is not fully developed, and the community is very poor. Fishing is the prime industry, and in some parts there is lumbering. During the month of September, 1935, it was estimated that the fishing industry lost over half a million dollars solely due to inclement weather. A fact such as this will enable readers to understand how badly the island has been hit by the depression.

The Newfoundlander is reputed to be very religious, and church attendance is fairly high. The strength of the individual denominations is of the following order— Roman Catholic, Anglican, United Church of Canada (composed of Presbyterian, Methodist and Congregational) and Salvation Army. There is little or no Baptist cause, and but a sprinkling of other connexions.

The Roman Catholicism of the island is of the best type. Most priests invite missioners to conduct seasonal "missions," and their parishioners are peaceable citizens living in harmony with their neighbours, the Protestant majority.

The Anglican Church is very strong, and there is an admitted *increase* of strength generally. The churches are well filled, and on special occasions, overcrowded. The parishioners are very loyal to church and clergy, the high financial contribution being an amazing thing in these days of depression.

The same story is largely true of the United Church— good attendance, loyalty, and deep religion. And of course the Salvation Army is making progress in many directions.

There is comparatively little desecration of the Lord's Day, and when families move out of the town to a summer residence, they usually make one trip that day to a city or country service. I imagine that the state of affairs is comparable to Ulster or perhaps Scotland in this respect.

The reader may have by now arrived at the conclusion that Newfoundland has no need of revival. After considering the foregoing facts, such a conclusion is forgiveable. But there are flaws in the perfect picture which upon examination reveal an unhappier state of affairs. There is, indeed, a position which calls for the deepest prayer for Newfoundland.

At the little conference with the ministers I made one discovery which threw light on the subject. After hearing about the commendable loyalty to the church as an institution, I ventured a question:

"And does the good attendance include meetings for prayer?"

"Er—well," said my informant, "you see, we all find that worship to-day is a different thing to worship a generation ago. Young people now-a-days express their loyalty to God in another way than prayer meetings and the habits of the old people. They show their worship in—say, social and cultural and educational activities, such as debating clubs, and the like."

"Admitting the value of such to young people," said I, "do I understand that these are indulged in to the exclusion of meeting with God in the place of prayer?"

"Well, personally, one has come to the conclusion that the—er—new method is better than the old method of last generation, and one feels personally that all efforts to change the social order are of greater importance than the out-of-date practices of the old-timers."

To quote the blunt assertion of a warm-hearted Evangelical:

"The majority of the churches don't have prayer meetings. And a great number of ministers preach politics, social work, anything but the real Gospel. They don't understand what you mean by revival. There are exceptions, mark you, ministers and groups of people who are heart-hungry for a real revival of real spiritual interest and work—but they are few."

A prominent minister and educationalist admitted to me:

"Yes, there is definitely something missing now-a-days. Thirty and forty years ago, there were revivals in the Methodist Church which swept the whole country. I believe that one of the strengths of those movements was the class meeting, where people met to tell of their experience of God and to receive instruction at the hands of a godly leader. Now all that has gone; nothing has taken its place: and there are no longer the revivals."

One of these ministers quoted a well-known author and preacher's prediction that we should never experience another revival until we had cleared up the crying social scandals. To which I replied:

"Without defining what is meant by the social implications of the Gospel of Christ, I *will* say that we need a revival to give us the enabling power to accomplish things in His name. God uses a minority to influence the community—and if that minority is composed of converted men and women, our task is to get more men and women converted."

And, sorry to say, the last-named business is not the main concern in Newfoundland churches. The masses are Gospel-starved. The trouble is caused by the lack of spiritual preaching and praying.

Turning thoughts for a moment to the state of the Anglican Church, another trouble shows itself.

"What," I asked the prominent Churchman with whom I had the cordial discussion, "would be the attitude of your communion here if, say, an evangelist already acceptable to Churchmen and non-Churchmen in Britain, were to come here for evangelistic work? Even if he were a Churchman himself, would you join with the Non-conformists in a campaign?"

"The answer is a decided no! We would have no more idea of united meetings of any description, with the Non-conformists than with the Roman Catholics. We have never had such, and we are definitely opposed to the idea. Mind you, we do not preach against the other denominations—there is friendly feeling. But none of our clergy ever preach for another denomination, and we do not ask other ministers to preach in our churches. The Bishop does not approve of it."

Scarcely a "Keswick" atmosphere! When we realise how imperatively necessary is the unity of the Spirit in preparing the ground for revival, we see how great an obstacle this is to a sweeping revival.

I really believe that the situation in the "Old Country" is more hopeful than in Newfoundland. In Britain to-day, there are many churches which possess a leader whose theology and preaching is of the "modern" but (alas) ineffective and out-of-date variety, and (strange paradox) these same churches possess a live group of young people who have, and glory in, a real experience. For such churches there is great hope. But in the island Dominion of Newfoundland, there is lacking the "youth element" on whom so much depends.

The United churches, I believe, would welcome real evangelism. The Anglicans would welcome separate work.

Three things one would recommend for Newfoundland are:—the commencement of a youth movement such as the Young Life Campaign; the visit of a Keswick deputation with a strong Anglican representation; and the formation of a prayer union with the object, prayer for revival in Newfoundland.

The Newfoundlanders are lovable, sincere, and religious people, deeply, *and not shallowly*, emotional. The response to a message of revival would be immediate and lasting. Britain has been voluntarily helping the people of the Dominion through the greatest depression in their history. God grant that many intercessors may come to the rescue, praying earnestly for spiritual revival in our oldest colony.

CHAPTER III

TRANS-MARITIME TRAVELS

BLUE sky and sparkling sunshine ushered in the morning of October 5th and greeted our arrival in Canada. As we sailed up the harbour, one could not help noticing the beauty of the place. I felt sure that I would enjoy Halifax and Nova Scotia.

After 2,500 miles across the Atlantic, the prospect of travel by land seemed too good to be true. But one had some regrets at leaving the ship whose hospitality had been so enjoyable. And a ship is a place where folks make new friends whose comradeship is missed. These were my thoughts as the s.s. *Newfoundland* berthed at Halifax, Canada's winter gateway.

Customs and Immigration officials proved as courteous and as helpful as one could desire. I noticed the eyes of the Immigration officer light up as he glanced at my Russian visa. Putting "two and two together" I spoke to him a few words in Russian, to his great delight, for he was a Ukrainian who had fought for Britain in the Canadian Forces during the war.

Halifax proved to be as pretty as expected. Most of the houses were wooden, but of a pleasing style and appearance. The public buildings were very tasteful, the railway station and hotel being the first to greet the eye. In the station I noticed some baggage lockers suitable for depositing my bags while I was busy in the city. But I wanted to leave them at the station for Montreal, thus avoiding a second deposit. So I called a porter.

"Is there another station in Halifax?"

"Yes, sir. There are two others—the Police Station and the Fire Station."

"You seem to know them well!" I retorted, leaving my baggage.

Walking along the street a moment later, I met a clergyman. "Speak to him," came the inward urge, but I neglected the opportunity and lost it. At the Y.M.C.A. I made enquiries . . .

"Yes," I was told, "there are several ministers in town who are what you would call interested in evangelism. . . ."

Several names were mentioned.

"And where does Mr. Herman live?" I asked, remembering one of them.

"Across the harbour in Dartmouth."

"Too far away," said I. "Is there a Salvation Army Captain?"

There was, but he was not in when I called to see him.

Half an hour later, I came across the old Cathedral church of St. Paul's, and was pleased with the evangelistic flavour of its notice board. A street car conveyed me quickly to the residence of its rector. I did not expect to be invited to preach, but I wanted to make a contact. The Ven. Dr. Savary received me and courteously answered all my questions in such a way

as to display his sympathy with the Evangelical cause.
He was also the clergyman whom I had met. I next
crossed the beautiful harbour to Dartmouth, searched
for Rev. Neil Herman, called on the Roman Catholic
priest by mistake and told him all about my personal
experience of God's grace to his evident pleasure and
interest—and finally was ushered into the drawing-
room of the Baptist minister whom I had been seeking.
To say that he showed interest would be understating
the case, and the cordial interview ended with an
invitation to preach on Sunday morning.

With this I was well pleased, so I returned to Halifax
with a light step and happy heart, spending the rest
of the day in exploring the city. Halifax was founded
about two centuries ago, by the British Government
of the day, as a fortress for defending Nova Scotia
against the French who were always stirring up the
Acadians to resist British rule. It has had an interesting
history, one tragic incident being fresh in the public
mind—the memory of the blowing-up of a ship loaded
with T.N.T.—deadly explosive, which literally blew up
the whole city, leaving the ruins to cover thousands of
dead and dying. Halifax is now a busy port, boasting
of over 60,000 inhabitants.

At the end of an interesting day, I made my way
down to the Salvation Army Hostel, looking for a
cheap bed. I had begun this Candian tour in quite
a modest way—with 2 dollars 50 cents and a ticket
to Montreal.[1] The Army Hostel was full, so I secured

[1] Credit to pass the Immigration Bureau was kindly supplied by
business friends in London, but this was not for use.

a bed in a little Chinese hotel at a modest charge of 50 cents. I killed three of the permanent residents of the hotel—but I have learned by now not to grumble, nevertheless making sure that none accompanied me on my travels elsewhere. The financial outlook was none too hopeful when I went to sleep, but the comfort of the words, "He shall silently plan for thee," made an easy pillow for the slumber of the night. I prayed for the comforts of a Christian home for the next night, and rose in the morning convinced that my petition had been heard.

"Are you coming back to-night?" asked the Chinese proprietor, when I had finished breakfast.

"No-o!" I replied.

"Leaving town?"

"Well, no," I answered. "I am staying with friends to-night," and I cannot think what made me add, "outside the city."

However, as the statement was made with no intent to deceive, I did not trouble to correct it. What did it matter anyway? I walked down to the Ferry, met Mr. Herman, accompanied him to West End Baptist Church, where I spoke on the subject, "The Dynamic Christ"—the pastor's announced subject for his own address—to an attentive congregation who showed every sign of response to the message.

As we were walking to the church, Mr. Herman conveyed a message by request. A certain Colonel Laurie had phoned him to ask him to tell Mr. Orr that he would like to meet him and be of service in any way possible.

"But how did he know that you knew me?" I asked, all the while thinking, "He shall silently plan for thee."

"That's a mystery, now that you mention it," replied the pastor. "How *could* he have known—I told no one."

"Where does he live?"

"On the Truro line. He suggested that you should phone him."

"That's where I am staying to-night," I thought.

While waiting in the Pastor's study at the church, I heard a knock, which was followed by the sudden entry of the pastor and two gentlemen.

"This is Colonel Laurie," said the pastor, introducing the older of the two.

"And this is Lieutenant Spencer," added he, bowing "my son-in-law."

"He shall silently plan for thee," I thought as I shook hands with the man whom I knew was to become my host that night.

"I am very pleased indeed to meet you both," said I, "and also a little bit curious to know how you know me."

"I am known to Mr. Lindsay Glegg, Captain Godfrey Buxton, and . . ."

"Well, then," I interrupted, "I am even more pleased to see you. But tell me how you learned of my visit to Halifax, and why you phoned Mr. Herman?"

"Well, you see, my sister noticed from *The Life of Faith* that you had sailed in the s.s. *Newfoundland*;

and we searched the papers at ten-thirty last night
to discover that the ship had arrived yesterday; and
then we telephoned Dr. Savary, who confirmed the
fact of your presence here; and at last we got into
touch with Mr. Herman, so here we are at your
service."

After the service another gentleman introduced
himself.

"My name is Smith, Mr. Orr."

"Glad to meet you," I returned, adding, "Let me
see—your name sounds familiar—I have friends of
that name."

"Yes," said the Pastor, "the story says that
when the people were being named, the list was
exhausted, so the name Smith was given to the Others
Unnamed."

"Oh, no," replied Mr. Smith. "I have a friend who
tells me that one time everyone was called Smith, but
as a punishment for evildoing, one and another's name
was changed to something else . . ."

"Well now," he went on, "I have a favour to ask.
To-day there is a conference of Y.M.C.A. leaders from
all over the Maritime Provinces. You could not have
come at a better time. We shall be delighted if you
would come along in an hour's time to address us.
You have a message that we need, and we can alter
the programme for you."

And of course I went. The message was well received, and the response was all that could be hoped for.
A local paper got the news mixed up, however, stating

that, "at the second dinner held at noon yesterday, the
two groups were addressed by Edwin Orr, of England,
China Inland Missionary, at present visiting in Halifax
en route for the Far East."!!!

At four o'clock, my kind host—he was my host after
all—motored me to his lovely home out in the woods
alongside an equally lovely lake. The beauty of the
scenery en route was a thing which defies pen to
describe. Folks in the "Old Country" have, no doubt,
heard of the grandeur and beauty of the Canadian
"fall." But it is a thing to be seen before it can be
even imagined. The vivid scarlet maple leaves appear
as a flame in the woods; the yellows and the browns and
the greens form a background for the brilliant blaze
of autumn glory—and truly it can be said that the
woods are brighter, and as vari-coloured as the
rainbow.

Colonel Laurie's estate—carved out of the woods by
the late General Laurie—is situated on a lakeside where
Mother Nature—intoxicated—has outshone herself in
creating beauty. I felt stirred by all that I saw. The
Lord knows the effect of landscape beauty on me,
and "silently planned" the tonic for me. Just as
much appreciated was the hospitality of the family;
the kindness and the comfort and the fellowship
introduced me to Canadian home life, and I cannot
forget it.

In the morning we went down to the foot of the
garden, signalled by hand to the Ocean Limited
Express, and watched the huge, heavy train brake-up
and come to a standstill. A handshake and a hurried

Good-bye . . . and the train set off again. All my needs had been wonderfully supplied—the little things and the big things too, and so as I sat in the train reiterating the promise, "He shall silently plan for thee," I could add the words, "He doeth all things well."

.   .   .   .   .

The Maritime Provinces of Canada form the Atlantic seaboard of the great Dominion, and are the oldest settled parts of it. The early French pioneers settled in Cape Breton Island, in Acadia, in the Isle of St. Jean, and other districts—all of which are included within the boundaries of the three Maritime Provinces —Nova Scotia, New Brunswick, and Prince Edward Island. In the great struggle between French and British for supremacy in North America, the French were finally defeated, and piece by piece their territory passed to the conqueror. But long before General Wolfe's famous victory over the gallant Montcalm on the Plains of Abraham resulting in the capture of the stronghold of Quebec, the part of Acadia known as Nova Scotia was won by the British. The French settlers, stirred up by their co-religionists of Quebec, continually gave trouble to their governors, leading to the deportation made notorious in Longfellow's "Evangeline." They filtered back again, and to-day there is a large French population scattered throughout the Maritimes. In the meantime, successive British settlements were made, culminating in the great migration of the United Empire Loyalists—composed of tens of thousands of Americans who were deported from the

c

United States for their loyalty to Britain. These latter settled in New Brunswick and founded the city of St. John. Since then, a fairly steady stream of British emigrants have reached the Maritimes. All these factors are worth remembering in considering the spiritual state of the provinces.

The area of the three provinces together, 51,000 square miles, is about one-sixth of the average area of the larger provinces of Canada. Prince Edward Island, known as the million acre farm, accounts for two thousand square miles, New Brunswick and Nova Scotia almost equally sharing the remainder. The population is a little over a million—or two-thirds the average population of the rest of the Canadian provinces, despite the fact that the number of people to the square mile is greater than anywhere else in Canada (P.E.I., 40; Nova Scotia, 25; New Brunswick, 15; Rest of Canada, 6). Consequently one may be forgiven for treating the Maritimes as one area—a practice already in vogue throughout Canada.

The strongest denomination in the Maritime Provinces is the Roman Catholic Church. In Prince Edward Island, the population is 88,000, of whom 39,000 are Romanists, 30,000 United Church of Canada, 15,000 Presbyterians (those who refused to unite), the remainder equally divided between Baptist and Anglican. In Nova Scotia, the 163,000 Roman Catholics are followed by 111,000 United Church, 88,000 Anglicans, 82,000 Baptist adherents, and 49,000 Presbyterians in a population of half-a-million. In New Brunswick, where the old Acadians are now settled, the Romanists form nearly one-half of the 408,000 people, the next strongest denomination being the Baptist (83,000)—accounted for by the preponderance of that persuasion among the United Empire Loyalists from the States, just as the numerical strength of the Presbyterians (both inside and out of the United Church) in Nova Scotia and Prince Edward Island is explained by the presence of settlers from Scotland and Ulster. The Anglicans are strong in the neighbourhood of Halifax and in Cape Breton Island.

So much for statistics. One of the first leaders with whom I had a discussion described the position spiritually as "just the same as prevails throughout the English speaking world—there is great need for improvement—and the same tragic indifference." In the United Church, the Presbyterians, and the Baptists, one learns that there are two chief classes—ultra-modernists who preach their theories, and lukewarm evangelicals whose gospel is spoiled by their "intellectual assent" to the liberal theology. It is commonly thought that a minister who holds to the fundamental truths is somewhat backward in intellect. Dalhousie, the great university, has had a full share, I understand, in creating this state of affairs. One learns that there is little to vie here with the programme of the I.V.F. in Britain. Something needs to be done. But of course there is a keen minority of Evangelicals in all these churches. There is little or no Anglo-Catholicism in the Anglican Church, but there is a certain amount of formalism. An Evangelical minister in a big Maritime town said to me: "I am as charitable as possible when I say that there is not another single church group in this town with whom I can have real fellowship. My Anglican confrères in the ministry are somewhat formalistic and 'starchy' and the others are simply leaders of social clubs. We certainly need a revival of spiritual religion."

There is great prayerlessness in the churches. This does not worry the leaders, who are more ambitious when it comes to enthusing their people with social and political fervour. All too few have got the right perspective—to wit, "preach the Word." Why? It is because too few can testify of a personal experience of Christ, and the majority of those who can and those who cannot have been utterly spoiled by their theological training.

And yet it is true that scores of leaders are really interested in revival. May God open their blind eyes to the causes of the decline—neglect of prayer, wobbly theology, scorn of evangelism, and the crime in making agnostics responsible for the training of candidates for the ministry.

In praying for revival, we should make the spearhead of our intercession the petition, "Lord, send a revival to the students." The effect of the witness of a score of such would be tremendous. In New Brunswick especially the people are wonderfully responsive to the preaching of the Word, but, oh, how few there are to preach it! In the other two provinces, the people are deeply religious though less likely to wear their hearts on their sleeve.

Is revival possible in the Maritimes? I believe it is. Revival begins with God's Holy Spirit, but demands human co-operation.[1]

The effectual fervent prayer of a righteous man availeth much.

[1] The following from a pamphlet is of interest: The application of the Evolutionary Hypothesis to all types of education has attacked the very core of Canadian Christian citizenship! This startling fact, well known to every thoughtful Bible believer, is being realized in a forceful way by those who occupy positions of leadership amongst Evangelicals. Faced by obstacles well-nigh insurmountable and problems impossible of solution by unaided human wisdom, they are experiencing the full shock of Satanic attack.

Especially in the Maritime Provinces does Church life lack spiritual power; ecclesiastical machinery all tends towards utopian social programmes; while the true life in Christ of the individual believer is parched, thwarted, and stunted because the very vitals of Christian experience are being eaten away by the deadly canker of Modernism. Lying adjacent to the New Brunswick border is the great Province of Quebec, its more than two million inhabitants almost completely under the control of Rome and the pagan interpretations of Scripture taught by the Papacy. The same domination obtains in Nova Scotia and New Brunswick, while about forty per cent. of the population of Prince Edward Island is Roman Catholic. The Protestant denominational movements, here as everywhere, are rapidly developing a rigid formalism of worship, "Modern" educational methods in Sunday School and Young People's work, an emphasis upon money raising for "missionary" enterprises of a purely social and educational type, and a secularization of Christian living. The result is utterly appalling, and renders real Biblical and spiritual Christianity entirely out of harmony with the general educational and social life of the Provinces. Everywhere there is a lowering of standards of morality and ethics, a destruction of home life in its Scriptural sense, and an absence of any vital message in either pulpits or educational centres.

In the universities, of which there are five, the general basis of all education being the Evolutionary Hypothesis, an attitude toward life has resulted which can only be described as materialistic. The issues are the present prevailing great apostate movements in Church life. These, being largely matters of indifference to the general public, have subtly caused Scriptural holiness of life to be dismissed entirely from the average person's practical experience. At the same time the existing religious and educational institutions are greatly venerated, huge sums being spent each year upon their perpetuation. Without misrepresentation or malicious motive it may be honestly said that *The Maritimes have a form of Godliness, but deny the power thereof.*

CHAPTER IV

THE PEOPLE AND PRIESTS OF FRENCH CANADA

THE weather continued to be favourable as I journeyed on, making my way from the Maritime Provinces to French Canada. I left Moncton at night and awoke as the train reached a French-speaking countryside, making possible the delusion that we had been mysteriously transported to Normandy. We kept south of the mighty and beautiful River St. Lawrence, reaching at last the town of Levis opposite the city of Quebec. The ferry boat took us across the wide, wide river, landing us at the foot of the great cliffs which gave their name to the city and province.

"Pardon, monsieur," said I to the first loiterer I met, "où est l'Hôtel des Postes?"

He directed me, and I proceeded by street-car to the General Post Office in the Upper town. Letters attended to, I commenced to spy out the town. How to make friends, where to sleep, and how to be of service, were three of the problems which became the subject of my prayers. They were soon answered. I introduced myself to the Y.M.C.A. secretary, who received me kindly, and invited me to speak at a meeting of "Y's men" after supper. For the space of time spent in Quebec, I lacked neither food nor lodging.

Another very happy contact was the meeting with Rev. A. C. Dixon, the minister of the English Baptist Church. His kindness was great. The third contact was equally happy. I traced the French Baptist pastor, and soon made my way to his home.

"J'ai rencontrai Madame Blocher à Paris, aussi Docteur Pache à Nogent," I explained to him.

"Oui? Bon! Entrez, monsieur," he said delightedly, and from that moment we were at home. I kept up the French conversation as long as I could, and found thereby how much he was interested in revival. My new friend came from Switzerland—as did his wife also—and knew many friends of mine. I passed on a copy of the little tract *La prière et le Reveil, par J. E. Orr*, which Pastor van Goethem of Belgium is so kindly circulating. Next followed an invitation to speak to the French Canadians at the Prayer Meeting. This I gladly did, speaking in both French and English, and we had a happy time, followed by a season of refreshing prayer.

The work among French Canadians in Quebec City was commenced in 1857 by Monsieur Normandeau— a converted priest. At first large numbers gathered to hear his message—doctors, lawyers, judges, and others —but priestly intervention scattered them. But at the end of ten years, he had a church of twenty members. The work has continued through many vicissitudes, and it is now a fine place.

Quebec City is a most beautifully situated place, rivalling Budapest and Constantinople in this respect. The upper town, built on the top of high cliffs, was regarded as the impregnable stronghold of North America. As I walked through the old town, and over the Plains of Abraham, I realised what an impossible thing Wolfe's victory was. The gallant French soldier, Le Marquis de Montcalm, defended the town against a besieging British army and fleet. After fighting, the place seemed as impregnable as ever. But one dark night, shipload after shipload of British soldiers drifted down with the tide to a spot now known as Wolfe's cove. Led by the Highlanders, they scaled the (so-called) impossible heights of Abraham, and spread themselves out in battle array on the plains above the town. Montcalm at first refused to credit the report carried to him, but seeing for himself, he gathered his troops and attempted to drive the British into the river. The battle raged furiously, but the day was won for the Empire. Wolfe was killed leading his men, and the equally brave Montcalm was carried from the field dying. Thus was decided the fate of North America.

Quebec City has always been the Vatican of the New World. To-day, out of a population of 130,000, only five thousand are Protestants. The city is also the true focus of French Canada. French culture and French religion are even more strongly entrenched than before the days of British conquest.

It must not be forgotten that the Roman Catholic missionaries who came out from France were idealists escaping from a corrupt old regime, eager to set up a New Jerusalem for the Church of Rome on the North American Continent. They were as brave as they were fanatical. For instance, when the Iroquois Indians captured Brebeuf, the founder of the Huron mission, they tortured him with all the diabolical cruelty for which they were noted. He was bound to a stake, and scorched from head to foot. Then they cut away his lower lip and thrust a red-hot iron down his throat to silence, not his cries, but his rebukes. That failing to make him wince, they hung around his neck a necklet of redhot hatchets. Still he would not cry out, so they poured boiling water upon his head, kettle after kettle. Failing again, they cut off strips from his legs and ate them before his eyes. Not a sign of pain he gave—winning the admiration of his cruel enemies, who then scalped him, drank his blood before he was dead, and devoured his heart so that they might partake of his heroic bravery.

Such was the determination of the early Jesuit pioneers. But they were as ruthless as they were brave, allowing nothing to stand in the way of the Roman Pontiff. And Quebec is still their stronghold. Everywhere one sees the droves of "men in skirts." The influence of the priest is paramount.

I know of one young French Canadian who professed conversion. The law of the Province of Quebec is not British law, but a modified form of the Napoleonic code. French Canadians are regarded as Romanists *by law*, and when one desires to change, he is compelled to publish a letter of abjuration, to send one to the Romish bishop, and another to the Protestant minister. Thus the whole machinery of the Church begins to work against him, for the Romanists do not hesitate to use the weapon of boycott. This young man sent his letter to the Bishop. By and by, a priest visited his place of employment.

"What is this? You have sent a letter to the Bishop, n'est-ce pas?"

"Oui, m'sieur le curé. And I mean every word of it, too."

"Imbecile. You cannot mean it. You would not be such a fool as to become a heretic, and leave Mother Church. Ce n'est pas possible, mon fils."

But the young man had already made up his mind. The priest gave it up and crossed over to speak to the manager. At the end of the week, the man was dismissed.

"Are you dissatisfied with my work, monsieur?"

"No. It is not that. You are my best worker."

"Had it anything to do with the visit of the priest?"

"Well, you see, yes. That is the reason."

The young man found employment with another firm in the same line, and the proprietor was a Protestant. But his Roman Catholic workmates mislaid his tools, played nasty tricks on him, made his work so impossible that he had to leave, emigrating to another country far away from the power of Rome. This is but one case among many to illustrate the methods adopted by Rome in Quebec to-day.

I was told in Quebec that the most useful work in the evangelisation of French Canada was being done by the Grande Ligne Mission. I left for Montreal, deeply regretting that its headquarters were too far away from my destination to permit of a visit. Arriving in Montreal next morning, I began my visit there with

much the same needs and prayers as in Quebec—
hospitality and useful service. In the same remarkable
way, I met a kindly and deeply spiritual minister, Rev.
J. A. Johnston of Westmount Baptist Church. Again
hospitality "dropped from the sky," and every other
need was provided.

"I have been thinking," said Mr. Johnston, "that
to spend your time most profitably, you ought to visit
the Feller Institute of the Grande Ligne Mission. It
is an awkward place to reach, but I will gladly motor
you out. What's that? Have you heard of it before?
So you were wanting to go—isn't that remarkable?"

We motored out one morning. I had the pleasure of
speaking to a fine body of students, French Canadians
chiefly—some of whom, no doubt, will be used of God
as their predecessors have been in the past, in the
evangelisation of French Canada. The Grande Ligne
Mission and its school, the Feller Institute, were
founded a hundred years ago by Madame Feller and
Pastor Louis Roussy. In the providence of God, the
revival which swept Switzerland under the ministry
of the revivalist Robert Haldane at Geneva, resulted
in the sending out of these two pioneers to French
Canada. The work began in a log cabin near St.
John's, Quebec Province, and grew amazingly.

"You will be glad to know," said the Principal to
me, "that this place was born in prayer, continued in
prayer, and has grown by prayer."

As the school prospered, so did the evangelistic
work; little company after little company was gathered
out, souls were won for the Lord, and a move was

made in the evangelisation of the Province. Pastor Roussy died in 1880, a dozen years after the passing of the saintly Madame Feller, and was succeeded by one of the Mission's pupils, Rev. Alphonse de L. Therrien, whose ministry was marked by many blessed revivals. Rev. G. N. Massé became principal of the school which then entered upon a new phase of development and success. An impartial critic told me that the Grande Ligne Mission was¦ the most blessed factor in the work of carrying the Gospel to the French Canadians. I thoroughly enjoyed my visit there, and felt hushed in spirit as I walked around the little God's acre where lie the earthly remains of those who have pioneered.

Rev. Mr. Johnston took me back again, or rather I took my turn at the wheel on the way to Montreal. It was also in his company that I went sightseeing in the city.

Montreal is the great metropolis of Canada, and the population of Greater Montreal exceeds a million. Some readers will be surprised to learn that the second largest French-speaking city in the world is Canada's commercial centre, Montreal, Paris being the first. Four-fifths of Montreal people speak French, and of course the city was founded by the French, being discovered by Jacques Cartier. It takes its name from Mount Royal, the hill in the middle of the island on which the city is built—the island being in the broad waters of the River St. Lawrence. It is hard to realise that Montreal, one of the great ports of the world, is 1,000 miles from the sea, but such is the case.

The spiritual position in Montreal is tragic. The city is overwhelmingly Roman Catholic, and little is done by the Protestant minority to witness for Christ to the majority. Roman Catholics do not hesitate to use the weapon of a boycott—and in consequence, many Protestants "lie low" in the matter of witness.

One of the tragedies of the Protestant churches of Montreal is the dearth of prayer meetings. The ensuing spiritual poverty is a part of a vicious circle—lack of prayer, lack of power, indifference, worldliness.

While I was in Toronto, I received a very cordial invitation from my new friend, Rev. J. A. Johnston, to come back again and take the Sunday services on the third of November. I left Ottawa for Montreal in due course and was met at the Bonaventure Station by one of the officers of Westmount Baptist Church. The pastor had informed me that he would be away taking other services, much to our mutual regret, but his helpers at the church made up for the loss of his great kindliness and sympathetic support by being equally good.

I went direct from the station to the parsonage, where there was a large gathering of keen young Christians. Several denominations were represented, and both the Inter-Varsity Christian Fellowship and the B.Y.P.U. had supplied strong contingents. The partitions between three rooms were removed, and we settled down in an exceedingly friendly atmosphere. From the commencement, it was evident that the Holy Spirit was working in our midst, and when the message and challenge had been delivered, there was a spontaneous turning to prayer. The petitions were all very personal and very brief—"Lord, take away the unbelief of my heart"; "Cleanse me from secret faults"; "Begin revival in my heart"; "Forgive my sin of prayerlessness." There was a deep sense of prayer. After this time of refreshing, I was eagerly cross-questioned by young folk who wanted to be practical. "What can we do to deepen the fellowship of prayer for revival in Montreal?" I told them what could be done, and was gratified at the response.

Next morning, the usual services were held. The morning service had a quiet dignity which I greatly appreciated, and the evening service had just the right degree of informality. Many were the personal testimonies given me, of blessing received from the hand of God. Westmount Baptist Church, and especially its young people, is one of the bright spots in the hope of revival in the great metropolis of Eastern Canada. The I.V.F. is another.

CHAPTER V

ONTARIO—THE BACKBONE OF CANADA

I ARRIVED in Toronto on October 12.

Seven months previously, I had been talking to a group of Latvian pastors gathered for a conference in the Salvation Temple in Riga, the headquarters of the Russian Missionary Society. These pastors were of various affiliations, supported by various missionary societies, working in various sectors of the field.

"Do you hope to go to Toronto some day, Brother Orr?"

"Yes, I expect so," I replied.

"Then you must not forget to look up Brother Oswald Smith."

"I have heard of him," I said; "and I think I have seen his books. But how do *you* know him?"

My friend appealed to the group standing around.

"How do *we* know Oswald Smith?"

They eagerly told me that this Canadian pastor had been wonderfully used of God in the evangelisation of Latvia.

"But how?" I asked. "He is not a missionary here."

"Well, you see. He supports a group of native missionaries on the field here, and his church has been a great help to Latvia."

"And is he interested in revival?"

A month later I read his book *The Revival We Need*.[1]
Had I read it before, that question would have been
unnecessary.

"He certainly is," my Latvian friend replied. "You
will find him a man after your own heart. You can
be sure that we will pray God to lead you to Brother
Oswald Smith's in Toronto. There are many, many
people in Latvia who pray for him night and morning."

"Well, thank you," I answered. "I'll pray that the
door may open. But I want to ask you a favour. You
won't write and tell Mr. Smith that I want to visit
his church?"

They promised not to write, greatly relieving me,
for I strongly dislike inviting myself anywhere. Their
prayers and mine were answered. On the day that
I reached London, I received a letter with a Canadian
stamp on it. It was from Rev. Oswald J. Smith, inviting
me to conduct meetings in his church. How did it
happen? A Canadian friend of my mother's, after
reading my first book, felt led to buy copies to send to
various ministers in Toronto, praying that this might
lead to an invitation to Toronto. The book reached
Mr. Smith as an anonymous gift.

As the train steamed into Union Station, Toronto,
I was wondering if there would be someone to meet
me. At the barrier I scanned the faces of the crowd,
but recognised none of them. My eyes were caught by
one, however, a medium tall man in a tweed coat,
keen-eyed, bareheaded.

[1] *The Revival We Need*, Oswald J. Smith (Marshall, Morgan &
Scott, Ltd.)

"I wonder is that Mr. Smith?" I thought.

This gentleman did not recognise me, however. I waited to see if someone else would turn up. Nobody else came, and the crowd began to disperse. I noticed that the gentleman remained. So I walked over to him.

"Are you Mr. Smith?"

"Ye—es."

It occurred to me that there would probably be quite a colony of Smiths in Toronto. So I said: "Well, my name is Orr."

He smiled. He had not recognised me. Next moment we were making our way to his car. Fifteen minutes later, he had me transported to my temporary home. I was beginning to like Toronto already. Jarvis—where I made my G.H.Q.—is a long street known by three different names. The lower section is in the business area and is called there "Jervis". The middle section is just plain "Jarvis". The upper part, being residential, is often called "Jahvis".

One of my first callers in Jarvis was a Doctor of Divinity, with whom I had quite a conversation. As I was seeing him to the door, he turned round and said:

"So you will be in Toronto for two weeks? Well, I hope to see more of you. Yes, I hope to see more of you."

"Sorry to disappoint you, Doctor. You won't see any more of me."

"No? Well, that's too bad."

"You see," I explained, "there isn't any more of me."

Toronto people are exceedingly likeable. There is a freedom about them seldom seen elsewhere. As one

D

would expect, they are proud of their fine city. They do not talk too much about "Tronna" as they call it. But nevertheless they are pleased to hear a stranger praise the city's merits.

Toronto has a population of over 825,000, and even in the days of depression it is a prosperous place. Situated on the shore of Lake Ontario, it stretches along the water-front for miles. There has been plenty of space to plan the city, and I found it a very easy city for getting around. Most of the streets run at right angles, Bloor (quite a dozen miles long) running east to west, and Yonge (longer still) south to north through the suburb of North Toronto. The streets are usually adorned by avenues of trees, which certainly beautify them. The houses in the residential areas are well set back in their own little gardens. There are no "slummy" districts. The business area is close by the water-front, which itself is not spoiled by ugly buildings, for Toronto has reclaimed much land from the lake and this has been given over to boulevards.

The Peoples Church, where I was expected to preach, is situated on Bloor not many yards from the corner of Yonge; and as these two streets carry most of the traffic, north, south, east, and west, the Peoples Church is perhaps the most accessible in the whole city. So much for the situation. The church's main auditorium itself holds 1,500 people and there are smaller ones for prayer meetings, inquiry rooms, classes, and the like. Even with this the accommodation is cramped, for the activities of the church are manifold.

One could describe The Peoples Church as an independent evangelistic-missionary work, standing for the essential truths of the Gospel. The missionary record of the place is amazing—the average amount raised each year for foreign missions (during the past five years) exceeds 30,000 dollars (£6,000). This in itself would be sufficient as a *raison d'etre*, for with this money considerable work is done in the border States of Russia, France, and Spain. The money itself is raised by monthly subscriptions and at an annual Convention— and these voluntary offerings were, at one time, supporting as many as seventy workers in various fields.

But The Peoples Church is also an evangelistic centre. Week by week, inquirers are dealt with, and the Gospel is preached to big audiences. People of all denominations come from all over the city. The membership is not rigid, but a large proportion of those who attend have made the place their spiritual home. But, of course, many who decide for Christ return to their own churches in other parts of the city, so that the influence of these efforts on Bloor Street is city-wide.

As one would expect, a great deal of the human part of the work centres around the pastor. A man of tremendous energy and restless spirit, Oswald Smith is certainly a factor in the Lord's work in Toronto. This year (1935) he celebrated the twentieth anniversary of his ministry in the city. He graduated from McCormick Theological Seminary, and was ordained to the Presbyterian ministry in 1915. The same year he was called to Dale Presbyterian Church as an associate pastor. After serving there for several years, Mr. Smith became identified with the Christian and

Missionary Alliance (founded by Dr. A. B. Simpson) and under his leadership a great Tabernacle, seating about 1,800, was erected, and this continued to be overcrowded service after service. Following this, Mr. Smith travelled extensively in evangelistic and missionary interests, returning to a Toronto congregation which is now meeting in The Peoples Church.

Most of these facts I had to collect from various sources, as the man himself proved reticent in making mention of his work for God. My own contact with him proved to me his evangelistic fervour, his wide missionary vision, and his emphasis on the deeper things in the Christian life. Of course, to a Britisher, some of the methods adopted were novel—but they were very effective. The opinion of one prominent leader of another denomination:—"Personally I praise God for what he is doing"—I recognised as a valuable tribute, just as I felt compelled to ignore the petty jealousy of small-minded men, happily few and very far between. No pen sketch of Oswald Smith would be complete without a mention of the fact that he is author of hundreds of hymns, many very well known, and author of books whose total figure of circulation exceeds 200,000.

The campaign opened on Sunday morning with the auditorium filled. I soon got adjusted to the temperament of the congregation, and found the utmost freedom in delivering the Lord's message. I found myself thanking God that there was no stiffness present. But when it came to the evening service, I was truly amazed. Long before the opening of the service, the church was packed out, dozens standing, and hundreds being turned away. The entire service was broadcast, reaching a vast unseen audience. It was my first time before the microphone, but I decided that the best thing to do was to ignore it, beyond noting when the little bulb flashed its signal that we were "on the air."

Rev. Oswald Smith's report stated: "J. Edwin Orr's first day in The Peoples Church was fraught with much blessing to thousands. He spoke both morning and evening as well as over the Back Home broadcast, and there were no dull moments. As usual the church was not only filled, but packed beyond capacity, hundreds being compelled to stand in the vestibule and aisles, while large numbers were turned away. Several were saved at the close of the service. Mr. Orr is a rapid speaker and quite different from the average visitor from Great Britain. His style is conversational, his voice strong, his enunciation clear, and he was heard easily by everyone.

"Mr. Orr's messages were simple and to the point, and he was in no way ponderous. The truth presented was heart-searching, and his narratives fascinating. He is humble, spiritual and humorous, natural Irish wit captivating his audience at once. We anticipate a time of spiritual blessing."

The radio ministry opened my eyes. Immediately after the service, the phone bell rang. I went to answer. . . .

"Is that Mr. Orr? . . . You come from Belfast, don't you? . . . Did you happen to live on the Ormeau Road? . . . Your father had a business just above the Ormeau Park? . . ." The answer to

all these questions being "Yes," my caller told me that
he had been listening to my address, and had thought
that I was an old neighbour of his; and when he announced his identity, I discovered that he was a family
friend of twenty years' standing.

Again the phone bell rang. My answers were something like this. "Yes. . . . I went to Ormeau Park
School. . . . You may have been a schoolmate,
but you had better tell me your name first. . . .
Well, I knew a fellow of that name who married my
chum's sister. . . . And it was you? . . . Sure,
I'll come up and see the baby. . . . All right, I'll
see you there."

On Thanksgiving Day, something went wrong at
the transmitting station, and for the whole period of
the service the telephone rang continuously. It certainly
convinced me of the value of radio broadcasting the
Gospel. And what of results? At a testimony meeting,
a man stood up to say that . . . "Mr. Orr will be
glad to hear that a young man listening in last Sunday
evening became convicted of sin and decided for Christ."
Letters reached me from several who had come to
climax of decision during the broadcast, and I received
verbal messages from folks in hospital, folks in the
country, folks many miles away.

The first week of the campaign was given to ministry
among Christians. I did not carry any "stock sermons,"
but developed the same theme as elsewhere—"Past
Revivals"—"The Need of Revival"—"The Hindrances
to Revival"—"Victory over Sin"—"Full Surrender"—
"The Filling of the Spirit"—"The Secret of Abiding"

—God truly answered prayer as the meetings progressed. At one of the aftermeetings, 300 people waited behind, and there was an amazing breaking-down. Sins were confessed with tears of penitence; prayers ascended to God, obviously prayers of the heart: half a dozen were on their feet praying at the same time, for the people seemed to forget that anyone else but God and the individual were concerned and consequently ignored the presence of the remainder. Time was forgotten—a very encouraging sign. And then, night by night, unconverted folks decided for Christ.

Another report of Mr. Smith's stated: "What time of refreshing from the presence of the Lord. It is surely heaven on earth . . . a spirit of revival permeates every service. . . . Mr. Orr, unlike many preachers and evangelists, makes the application throughout,—drives home his points one after the other, and does not tack on the application at the end. He speaks of the sins of gossip, dishonesty, prayer-lessness, unbelief, impurity, criticism, etc. . . . being not only scholarly but logical in presentation of truth. The aftermeetings are becoming so large that it is necessary to stay in the main auditorium. Very few leave . . . the people desirous of spiritual blessing being in no hurry to go home. The message is clearly the Keswick teaching which has been such a blessing to untold thousands. Mr. Orr's diction is almost perfect, and he has an unusual vocabulary."

After one of these aftermeetings, a fine little Welsh-man came up.

"This reminds me of the Welsh revival, when I got saved. Now I want your prayers and your help, if you please. I am going off to California to hold a revival."

"Well," said I, "take my advice and don't try to *hold* a revival. Let it go. . . ."

The afternoon Women's meetings were splendidly filled, and the prayer meetings began to show an upward trend. One of the best things in the Peoples Church is the presence of scores of trained and experienced soul winners—the evangelist may turn over with confidence all inquiry-room cases to be dealt with by sympathetic, capable workers.

In the meantime, I was certainly enjoying Toronto. The people were exceedingly kind—so kind as to be cruel. Time and time again Mr. Smith, as an old campaigner, warned me not to accept too many invitations out, but I had not the heart to refuse. It was delightful to become acquainted with Toronto people in their own homes. They are surely the kindest of people.

I have one grumble to make. The first time I was out to lunch, my hostess told me that "as a special treat, they had provided me with pumpkin pie." *It was delicious.* And that evening for supper, another family offered me pumpkin pie. *It was fine.* I certainly enjoyed it as much as my hosts, for pumpkin pie is regarded as the season's delicacy. Each meal I had was with a different family—and so, with some exceptions, each did its best to give me the choicest dish, invariably choosing pumpkin pie. And so it was— I had pumpkin pie for lunch, dinner, supper. It even haunted my dreams. Of course, the first time it was delicious; the second time, it was fine; the third time it was very nice; the fourth time, it was good; the fifth time, it was all right; the sixth time, it was not so bad; the seventh time, it was *pumpkin pie*: the sixteenth time—what more shall I say? If it had not been for the lovely people who produced it, it would have been torment. A certain minister (from another city) wrote regarding my arrangements, and asked some questions about my services. He must have received a mild surprise when I telegraphed via Canadian Pacific "*No pumpkin pie.*" I hope that none of my Toronto hostesses are upset by reading this. On one or two or even three occasions, the quality was so superb that I really relished it. *It may have been yours.*

An Irish friend phoned me up.

"What about coming up to our house for a meal?"

"Excuse my rudeness, old fellow. Wild horses could not drag me out to any more meals. I am literally booked up to the limit."

"All right. Would you come to breakfast if we had an Irish fry?—fried potatobread and soda farls?"

I hired a taxi and went.

But I was really glad to have so many demands upon my (meal) time. What grand people they were, those Toronto people. I found it impossible to be lonely. And they made me so much at home. Instead of expecting to be entertained, they would show me to a quiet little corner, saying, "You ought to have a little time of rest and quiet." Or on other occasions, we had a sing-song at the piano (one of the finest tonics known to me), or perhaps a conversation in very congenial company.

One remarkable feature of Canadian city life as a
whole is the high indoor temperature. For me a temperature of 60 degrees Fahrenheit is quite warm, but
not so with the Canadians. They must have 70, 75,
and 80 or else they are grumbling about the cold. They
say of course that the extremes of temperature out-
doors require high temperatures indoors. But the truth
is that they wear summer clothes indoors in the middle
of winter, and put on extremely heavy overcoats when
going out. If they were to wear more next the skin
and keep a lower indoor temperature, they would be
able better to stand the cold. The hot Canadian
summer, and the hotter (indoor) Canadian winter
together *thin* the blood, thus undermining resistance
to the cold. It is an admitted fact that a newcomer
from the Old Country can stand the cold much better
than the Canadians themselves. Indeed many Old
Country people go out into zero temperatures without
even an overcoat. But after two summers and winters,
they become Canadianised—their blood gets thin on
account of the terrific indoor heat.

I had the pleasure of speaking at other meetings
arranged for me in Toronto. One of the first of these
was the Saturday night meeting of the Inter-Varsity
Fellowship, at which the Lord spoke to all of us. The
next meeting with students was at the Toronto Bible
College—and again I felt great liberty in addressing
them. Then there was the Railway Mission Conference
at which there seemed to be a real breaking down; I
was much impressed by the earnest plea for revival made
by Dr. Albert Hughes immediately after my address.

One of the most hopeful omens for the future was the unanimity and spontaneity of purpose displayed at the luncheon on the Saturday before my departure. Thanks to the kindness of Rev. Oswald Smith, we were able to arrange this very happy event at the shortest notice. Rev. Dr. McElheran, Archdeacon in the Anglican Church and Principal of Wycliffe College, presided over a most representative body. These ministers and leaders plied me with questions and were intensely practical in making suggestions. They agreed that the spirit of fellowship in prayer for revival in Canada was growing and that they had a real responsibility in the matter. I was most pleased to see them in such agreement, and was thankful when they formed themselves into a body responsible for carrying on the work of deepening prayer interest throughout Canada.

From the perverted Irish point of view, I enjoyed a great deal of amusement when the run on my books commenced. One enterprising firm had laid in a huge stock of the three volumes, as did also the Peoples Church. Within a matter of days, it was impossible to procure copies anywhere. Cablegrams traversed the Atlantic, another big supply came in response and disappeared just as quickly, leaving the booksellers to take orders. I was somewhat surprised to learn that 5,000 of my books were sold in Toronto.

My happy stay in Toronto was coming to a close. The attendances were increasing, so Mr. Smith suggested taking the great Massey Hall which seats 3,000 people. We arranged a farewell meeting there for my last Sunday night. The place was filled. It was in that vast auditorium that I saw Oswald Smith, the leader, at his best. He was an adept in handling vast crowds. Some of my closer friends were doubtful about the strength of my voice. They got a surprise, and one of them remarked, "Mr. Orr weighs one hundred and twenty pounds. He must be all voice."

An amusing thing happened that evening. Mr. Smith had announced that it was to be "Irish night"—so he appealed to the meeting.

"All of you who were born in Ireland and proud of it, stand up."

A thousand people stood up.

"Well, *what* do you *think* of *that*?"

Everyone laughed.

"And now, all who are of Irish parentage, stand up."

Another thousand rose to their feet, leaving a thousand sitting and looking very ashamed of themselves! Mr. Smith turned to me.

"Well, Brother Orr—you aren't the only Irishman in Toronto."

There are more Ulster folk in Toronto than any other class. (The Scotch run second, of course.)

On one occasion, after a long queue of people had shaken hands with me, each explaining what part of Ulster was "home," a lady said to me:

"Oh, Mr. Orr—I would like to shake hands with you, but I'm not Irish."

"Never mind," said I. "That isn't your fault—you couldn't help it."

My accent has been modified somewhat since I left Ireland, but in Canada and especially Toronto, I lapsed

into the broad, rich, expressive tongue of the North
of Ireland. The presence of so many countrymen
explained it.

It was with real admiration that I watched Eldon
Lehman, the Musical Director of the Peoples Church,
throw himself wholeheartedly into the task of leading
the great congregation in praise. His leadership of
the fine choir and orchestra was splendid, but it was
a greater achievement to weld together the voices of
3,000 individuals and lead them in inspiring singing,
thus preparing the way for the message.

At last the meeting came to a close. Workers were
dealing with those who waited behind. A girl came up
to me, shook hands, and was gone in a moment. But in
the interval she had said, "I am in service, so I cannot
wait behind. I am not saved. Will you pray for me?"

Rev. Oswald Smith reported that "the campaign
closed Sunday night with a great farewell service
in Massey Hall. Mr. Orr was clearly heard by everyone present as well as by a vast radio audience, for
the entire service was broadcast to multiplied
thousands. Toronto has been deeply stirred by these
meetings during the past two weeks. Unusually
large crowds gathered night after night in the
Peoples Church, members of all denominations
attending. Although he is not an evangelist in the
strict sense of the word, souls were saved at almost
every meeting. The message was primarily to
Christians, the note of revival being sounded throughout the entire campaign. Many were deepened in
their Christian experience. Mr. Orr left Toronto
with the love of the people and the prayers of God's
children following. All were captivated by his native

wit and humour, and everyone marvelled that one so young could have accomplished so much. We sincerely trust that God may send him back to Toronto."

The Lord's hand was seen in the campaign, and this explains the degree of blessing which resulted from the preaching of the Word. Oh that one were more yielded, more prayerful, more faithful—what could not be done! I was greatly challenged by a phrase from one of Rev. T. Gear Willett's letters: "May the Lord hold and use you, keeping you under His mighty hand, ever leading you lower and lower before the wondrous throne of grace—that He may lift you higher in the knowledge of Himself."

Satan's snares are so subtle that I have sometimes found myself wishing for the earlier days of my ministry, when persecuted and penniless, I had no one but God upon whom to throw myself. "Lower and lower in the things of self—higher and higher in knowing the Lord." That's the best ambition one can have.

A lady in Hamilton was sitting upon a park seat reading aloud to a companion. The book happened to be "Can God?" A man who had sat down at the end of the seat began to fidget, so the lady said to him:

"If this reading is annoying you, I'll stop."

"To tell you the truth, Madam, I was going to ask you if I might sit beside you while you read more."

God's Spirit was at work. The man decided for Christ before they got very far. This was the story told me by a lady who seemed anxious that I should visit her home city. So I promised to go.

The visit to Hamilton proved to be a very happy

one. Hamilton is one quarter the size of Toronto—
150,000 inhabitants. Delta Tabernacle was the venue
of the meetings—three in all. The Pastor, Mr. Holling-
rake, was a kind host and the people were equally
cordial. I also visited the city of Stratford. The *Stratford
Beacon-Herald* gave a lengthy report under the heading:
"Youthful Speaker Interests Audience in Ontario
Street Baptist Church Last Evening," and it mentioned
that I was staying with my uncle, Mr. W. Bradshaw.

Next followed a meeting in the Tabernacle in London,
a city of 75,000 people. This building was in the course
of erection. But the room which we used held about
500 people, and we had this accommodation crowded.
There was great blessing in the aftermeeting, one and
another in prayer confessing shortcomings, unbelief,
prayerlessness, secret sin, and other hindrances to individual revival. There was a significant disregard of time.

With Mr. Smith, I also paid visits to Peterborough
and Niagara Falls, but did not speak there.

A friend motored me up to Ottawa, the capital of
the Dominion, still within the boundaries of Ontario.
The meetings there were in the Christian and Missionary
Alliance Tabernacle at the corner of Bank and Rosebery
streets. This tabernacle is quite a large building,
its auditorium seating over 2,000 people. The meetings
were well attended, and there was a deep spirit of
earnestness in the gatherings. A church official wrote
to me "regarding the two inspiring meetings you spent
with us, our only regret is that your sojourn has been
so short. We sincerely hope that the Lord will see
fit to have you return to us at a later date."

Rev. D. C. Kopp is doing a fine work as pastor here, having recently returned from Congo Belge. He and I witnessed together the arrival of John Buchan, Baron Tweedsmuir, the new Governor-General of the Dominion of Canada. It was a fine reception that the Canadians gave him. The city was decorated with Union Jacks, and a salute of twenty-one guns was fired. Ottawa reminds me of Edinburgh, and yet it is quite different. It is a busy place, population 127,000, with a French-speaking section.

I was greatly impressed by the loneliness of Northern Ontario as I passed through on my way out west. Forests stretching as far as the eye could see, wild countryside, occasional clearings, settlements few and far between, and rocky, barren soil—thrown together and beautified—such makes up Northern Ontario. What a contrast to the settled lands of Southern Ontario.

The little peninsula of land between Lake Huron and Lake Ontario is the real backbone of Canada. When one looks at the map of that vast sub-continent, Canada, Southern Ontario looks insignificant. But it is the most important part of the great Dominion. Growing cities are scattered at regular intervals within its boundaries, and its capital is that fine city, Toronto. In Southern Ontario are found the best highways in the Dominion. Here also is the biggest concentration of population. Montreal may boast of its million, but Montreal has not got the hinterland possessed by Toronto. Southern Ontario is more British than Montreal is French. Southern Ontario is more Protestant than the Montreal district is Romanist.

Southern Ontario ranks in one's mind with Ulster for its Evangelical fervour. Like Ulster, it possesses an Orange Order as the spearhead of its militant Protestantism: and again, like Ulster, there are many who are more than *political* Protestants. The Anglican Church in Canada is remarkably like the Church of Ireland in its freedom from Anglo-Catholicism. The Free Churches exert much the same influence as their Ulster counterparts.

Taking the figures for the whole province, the population of Ontario is 3,431,000, one-third of Canadian population. The United Church of Canada is the largest denomination numerically, and one quarter of Ontario's population belongs to this church, which itself is an amalgamation of Methodist, Congregational and Presbyterian bodies. One regrets to remark that the United Church is reputed to possess the greatest proportion of leaders who hold liberal theological views. There are such men in the Presbyterian Church (half a million adherents) and in the Baptist Communion (171,000) but not to the same degree. The Anglican Church has three-quarters of a million adherents, being second in numbers, and the Roman Catholic Church possesses almost the same numerical strength. The Salvation Army is comparatively strong in Ontario.

And what of spiritual conditions? Again the strange likeness to Ulster is noted. Ontario is possessed of a virile, Evangelical Protestantism which has known better days. But there is more liberalism in Ontario than in Ulster, and the former has never had such a movement of the Spirit of God as the latter had in 1859. Toronto is rather like Belfast minus the Falls

E

Roman Catholic Area. It is the most Evangelical city in Canada, as Belfast is in the British Isles. The church attendance is good. There are no public houses or cinematograph shows open on Sunday. There is the same absence of Anglo-Catholicism. Toronto is often called "Toronto the Good," for there is much for thankfulness in its civic life.

But there is a great need of revival. Owing to the growing "deadness" of many churches, people outside the regular evangelical congregations are unreached by the Gospel. Many centres continue to be aggressive in their witness, but their influence is felt within a limited circle of adherents. In the Evangelical camp itself there is good co-operation between people of various denominations, but there is also petty jealousy between some leaders. One of the first signs of revival in Toronto will be the healing of such breaches between several leaders, breaches which are known to the majority of Christian people, and which hinder and hurt the work of God. Why they occurred one cannot say. But if the parties concerned were anxious for an awakening, they would not hesitate to proclaim aloud their unity instead of allowing their disunity to be whispered around the town.

There are many Evangelical people in Southern Ontario who feed on the best of good things. Outside their gates are Gospel-starved masses. Only a revival will change things. Thank God, the most hopeful sign in Ontario is the expectancy and anxiety of many of God's choicest saints for a revival straight from the presence of the Lord. I believe that the Lord will hear their prayer. Therefore we may expect a revival in Ontario before long.

CHAPTER VI

MANITOBA—THE THRESHOLD OF THE WEST

LORD DUFFERIN, on the occasion of his visit to Winnipeg in 1877, made a statement which gives the reader a glimpse of the importance of the province of Manitoba:

"From its geographical position and its peculiar characteristics, Manitoba may be regarded as the keystone of that mighty arch of sister provinces which spans the entire continent from the Atlantic to the Pacific. It was here that Canada, emerging from her woods and forests, first gazed upon her rolling prairies and unexplored North-West, and learnt as by an unexpected revelation that her historical territories were but the vestibules and antechambers to that, till then, undreamt of Dominion, whose illimitable dimensions confound the arithmetic of the surveyor and the verification of the explorer."

The first colony in the area now known as Manitoba owed its foundation to the genius of Lord Selkirk. This enterprising Scotsman began to see the great possibilities of the far-western territories. Until 1812, the only inhabitants of these vast areas were a few trappers, half-breeds, and Indians. Lord Selkirk's first party of settlers arrived at Red River in 1812, and the colony was set up. But the interests of the new settlement and those of the fur traders began to conflict, and bloodshed ensued. But Selkirk persisted. Everything seemed against him, and in 1820 he died in France. Canada must never forget that this great pioneer predicted—as early as 1816—that the Canadian West "might afford ample means of subsistence to more than thirty million British subjects." Time has abundantly justified Selkirk's faith. His prophetic vision saw first the great possibilities of the western country as the granary of the Empire.

Eventually, the Province of Manitoba was formed, a government being set up in 1871. The insurrections of Louis Riel—a half-breed—were the chief incidents of Manitoba's early history. Then the Province began to grow. Its population in 1868 was about 12,000, composed of less than 2,000 whites, the remainder being half-breeds. The population to-day is over 700,000.

This increase of population is accounted for by emigration. English-speaking settlers from Eastern Canada and the United States began to pour into the country; an Icelandic settlement was formed on the shores of Lake Winnipeg; in 1875, 6,000 Russian Mennonites of German origin settled along the Red River, and until 1930, their compatriots continued to follow them; then came new streams of emigrants from Britain. Seventy years ago, Winnipeg had a population of 7,000; and to-day Winnipeg's population is a quarter of a million.

Over one quarter of the population of Manitoba is Roman Catholic—chiefly of French and Irish origin. The United Church of Canada has 176,000 adherents, the Anglican communion 128,000, the Presbyterians and the Baptists sharing most of the remaining Protestants. The state of affairs spiritually is much the same as in other parts of Canada. Many of the churches which are still evangelical in name have lost the fire. Many others have lent too willing an ear to the seductive calls of present day liberalism. With them, the social gospel has replaced the gospel of individual conversion.

I heard an amusing story of an evangelist who visited Winnipeg some years ago. The battle against Nature in the raw has produced many very rough types of humanity; and it is not surprising that some of the Christians were of the same mould—rough, uncut diamonds. The evangelist who visited Winnipeg was one such, but the church in which he was speaking was of the ultra-fashionable type. They were rather shocked. I heard the story first-hand.

"My dear friends," said the evangelist, "I believe that we should share as much as possible, the life of our countrymen. I will give you an example. As I was walking along the street, my friends, I passed a lumberyard, and there I saw a big fellow buck-sawing a log of wood. Well, dear friends, my heart went out to that big fellow—what a grand trophy he would make, I thought.

"So, my friends," went on the evangelist, "I walked over to him and said to him, 'Wouldn't you like to give your heart to the Lord?' But the man replied: 'Oh, go away. Could you buck-saw a log of wood? If you could, I might listen to you.' Well, dear friends, I stripped off my jacket, took that-there buck-saw, and sawed that-there log of wood, and when I finished,

I said to him, 'Now, wouldn't you like to give your
heart to the Lord?' But he replied, 'Look here, if you
don't go away and stop your talk, I'll give you the
biggest licking you ever got.'

"That being the case, dear friends, I took off my
jacket again in all friendliness and fraternity, and I
gave *him* one of the biggest lickings that *he* ever got.
And after we had finished, my hearers, he gave his
heart to the Lord."

Although this story is true, it is not given as advice
to personal workers. It illustrates how much of the
spirit of the pioneer enters into the life of the man of
the prairies.

I arrived in Winnipeg on the 6th November. The
ground was snow-covered, there having been 35 degrees
of frost the night before. I left my baggage at the
station, walked up to the General Post Office, and
attended to correspondence. After breakfast, I telephoned Mr. Bellingham, the pastor of Elim Chapel,
a big church situated on Portage Avenue. He was
expecting my arrival and had arranged meetings in
the church.

Elim Chapel, an undenominational free church, has
long held the reputation of being one of the most
spiritual centres of witness and worship in the city.
It would be rather hard to define its church order
—I would describe it as partly Presbyterian, partly
Brethren. A prominent Winnipeg business man,
Mr. Sidney Smith, has been associated with the work
for many years: and another business man, Mr. John
Bellingham, recently gave up his business connections

to give his full time to the work of the pastorate. The spiritual contribution of these two men has greatly helped to make Elim Chapel what it is, and under their wise leadership, the blessing of the Lord has been fully enjoyed. The quiet dignity of the services appealed to me: and the people were of the best type. Like the Peoples Church in Toronto, Elim Chapel has a voluntary, fluid membership, and a great proportion of those who attend make the place their spiritual home. At ten o'clock each Lord's Day morning, there is an "open" Communion service.

It was in such a place that I was invited to minister the Word. On the first evening, despite bitterly cold wind and weather, there was a very gratifying attendance, and an equally gratifying response to the message. The attendances continued to be good, and in the three Sunday services they increased. The last service, Sunday evening at 7 p.m., was crowded—about 1,500 having gathered to listen to the message. Scores of people came to speak with me afterwards, telling me how the Lord had blessed them, and at the last moment I was dealing with some of those who desired to give their hearts to the Lord.

I enjoyed the visit to Winnipeg. The people are in some ways different to the Toronto people, but nevertheless they are very kindly and hospitable. The city has grown from a hamlet of thirty houses in 1870 to a fine big city, well planned and covering a large area. During my stay there, I journeyed out to the Canadian National Railway workshops in the company of a big Dutch emigrant and friends, and we had a meeting in one of the workshops—the men listened well. But there is great need of continued Christian witness such as the infant Railway Mission is endeavouring to give, for there appears to be a strong tendency to Communism among the railway workers.

When I was in Toronto, I received a letter from Vancouver:

"DEAR MR. ORR,
"I have just heard that you have arrived in Canada from England to hold evangelistic services throughout the Dominion. Have you got all your time booked up? Would it be possible to stop over in Brandon, Manitoba, for even a couple of days? I feel that Brandon needs a tremendous shaking. It is a city of 18,000 inhabitants."

The letter was signed by a name which sounded vaguely familiar. I studied my maps, and my diary, and decided to write and explain that pressure of work forbade any possibility of stopping off, even for a day, in Brandon. But it was arranged otherwise. Someone came up to me after a service, with the words, "I'll be praying for your visit to Brandon," whereupon I asked, "And how did you know that I was considering going there?" My friend immediately rejoined: "Well, I have heard from a friend in Brandon that a little circle of people have been asking the Lord to send you there, and you yourself say that God answers prayer."

So instead of sending the letter intended, I wrote another, saying that I hoped to be in Brandon from 12.40 p.m. Monday till 12.50 p.m. Tuesday, and accepting in anticipation any meetings arranged. A letter came back and stated: "I rejoice greatly that you can come. I have arranged a Women's meeting in the afternoon, women of all denominations will be there. And then at night we shall have the biggest church in the city, whose minister is very interested as are other ministers."

The name again struck me as vaguely familiar, so I made inquiries. I found that Miss Lillian Crawford, my Brandon correspondent, had studied singing at Toronto, London and Paris, having been successful in gaining many musical honours. But the Lord was interested in using that lovely singing voice, and at a conference at High Leigh in England, Miss Crawford came to know Christ as Saviour. The voice was given over to the Lord's use, and now the human owner was working for the Master in her birthplace, Western Canada.

Miss Crawford had stated that someone would meet me at the Canadian Pacific Railway Station. When I arrived I noticed quite a number of people who were meeting the train, and I selected one gentleman as the most likely one to meet me. But he just gave me a glance, and took no further notice. Dr. H. R. A. Philp once wrote in a word of commendation that the author was "a young Irishman whom no one would notice in a crowd." It has been both amusing and provoking to prove the truth of those words. I have known cases where people had refused to believe that I was I—much to my amusement and their embarrassment; but Brandon was not such an extreme case as this, and the gentleman accepted my word that "I was I." Miss Crawford then joined us and gave me a further surprise.

I had stupidly imagined that such a well-travelled lady must belong to an older generation, but instead she was a contemporary.

The Women's meeting was well attended, and there was much blessing. The evening service was well-attended also, surprisingly so—according to Miss Crawford. We had another service for young people from 9.30 p.m. till nearly 11 p.m. The Lord's presence was very manifest in that gathering. These meetings and various conversations gave me an insight into the spiritual condition of the smaller prairie cities. In Brandon there are several active Christian leaders, but it is true to describe the place as spiritually asleep. A little group of praying people which includes a couple of ministers, is holding on for revival. Miss Crawford's own efforts also in preaching and singing the gospel message are very deserving of prayer support. But humanly speaking, what are so few against the paralysing work of the majority who put their hope in a social gospel or exist in inactivity? Many of the churches are social clubs without evangelistic endeavour, and the Christian who is interested in soul-winning and spiritual life almost despairs. But the God of battles is with those who pray.

The hopeful sign in the outlook in the Province of Manitoba is found in the small but growing number of intercessors who are praying for revival and are willing to be channels themselves. They are intensifying their prayers and efforts in view of the Coming of the Lord Jesus Christ. Unfortunately, *this* great theme and assertion is either neglected or contradicted in Manitoban places of worship. More and more, one regards the colleges as being the chief cause of the decline, the chief channel through which the Devil deceives the very elect. Intercessors should always remember to pray for revivals among students; and the answer to such prayer is demonstrated by the records of the Inter-Varsity Fellowship.

The prayer of Daniel rings in my mind: "O my God, incline Thine ear and hear: open Thine eyes and behold our desolations—O Lord, hear; O Lord, forgive; O Lord, hearken and do; defer not for Thine own sake, O my God."

CHAPTER VII

SASKATCHEWAN AMID THE PRAIRIES

THE River Saskatchewan gives its name—which in an Indian tongue means "Swift-flowing"—to the Province of Saskatchewan, the middle prairie province of the west. The South Saskatchewan River rises in the Rockies, flows across Alberta, bends to the north, joins the North Saskatchewan River which also rises in the Rocky Mountains, and together they empty themselves into the Lake Winnipeg, from which the waters escape to Hudson Bay via the Nelson River.

In area the Province more than equals the two neighbouring American States of Montana and North Dakota. Saskatchewan is so rich in wheatfields, that for the average mind outside the province, it is not easy to think that it possesses anything else. But it is far from being a flat expanse of prairie. There are fine lakes, lovely rivers, forest reserves, and growing cities. The province is famous for its grain, and a great proportion of its population work the land. The actual population of Saskatchewan is approximately one million. Like Manitoba, the biggest section of the settlers are of Anglo-Saxon stock, but there are likewise other groups —the Scandinavian and German emigrants being both useful and popular.

One interesting settlement is that of the Doukhobors that strange sect from the steppes of Russia. These people were being persecuted by the (Czarist) Russian government, and the Canadian Immigration authorities decided to admit them to the prairies, giving them absolute freedom to carry on in their own communal mode of life. Troubles multiplied, for these queer people objected to registration of births, marriages, deaths, and all the other necessary regulations insisted upon by the Government. Certain of them felt impelled to revert to the Edenic civilisation—that is, to discard all clothing. A party of them marched through the streets of a Canadian city one New Year's Day—the remarkable features of the parade being the fact that it *was* cold and that the party was naked. But these folk are at last settling down to normal life—much to the relief of the Canadian authorities.

Regina is the capital of the Province and it is a busy city of about 60,000 inhabitants. It was here that I made my first stop-over in the province. The city has often been described as the "Queen City of the Plains," for it is situated in a land of thrilling spaciousness, a boundless, rolling plain of fertile soil. In the late summer, this plain is made more beautiful by the limitless, waving grain. The clear air—wonderfully clear—lays a spell upon the visitor to the prairies.

I did not know anyone when I arrived. I introduced myself to a distant relation living in the city, and both he and his family were most kind. I met also a minister, who was a very nice fellow, but who did not believe in the Resurrection of the body, the Virgin Birth of Christ, the Inspiration of the Scriptures, the Return of our Lord, and other important doctrines. I learned a few of the things in which he did believe, but they did not impress me much. So I said good-bye to this extremely nice fellow, not a bit surprised that he did not ask me to preach for him.

And so it was. Until six o'clock of the evening of the day of my departure, I had made no useful contact of the kind that I desired. I did have a nice chat on the phone with a Salvation Army officer—our mutual admiration of Hugh Redwood was the starting point of our fellowship. But the Army corps were pre-occupied with an important rally. Finally, my "distant relation" suggested that I should phone another minister whose name had just occurred to him. This man, an American, at first had the idea that one of the boys was playing a joke upon him; but the upshot of it all was that I was invited down to address his prayer meeting. What a wonderful prayer meeting it was. It meant much to those present—a new dedication of life and service— and we experienced times of refreshing from the presence of the Lord Himself.

At midnight I left for the city of Saskatoon, and arrived there to find fifty degrees of frost. Cold? It certainly was cold. As usual, I went to the Post Office first, had some breakfast, walked around, went back to the station again, out of the cold. I discovered that I was running short of financial resources, so I did not go to a hotel as I had done in Regina. Instead, I prayed for hospitality. I made mental notes as I wandered round the city until about eleven o'clock. Only twenty-eight years ago, Saskatoon was a village of tents, population 113 people, founded by the Barr colonists.

It is now a progressive young city of about 50,000. Its citizens have spared no efforts to make the place attractive, and there are fine streets and good buildings. On the east side of the river is the University of Saskatchewan, one of the finest on the continent.

Some time before arriving in the west, I had heard of the evangelical zeal of the Bishop of Saskatoon, so I decided to telephone him for an interview. There was no answer to my phone call, and no answer the second and third times. I discovered later that the Bishop was in England. Quite close, in the telephone book, to the Bishop's name was the name of the Principal of the Anglican College of the University campus. When he answered, he explained that he had just come out in the middle of a lecture to look for something.

"Will you please telephone again?"

Having nothing else to do, I walked through the city, over the 23rd Street Bridge, plodding my way through the snow to arrive at a convenient time to see the Principal. The charm and spirituality of the man, so apparent through his personality, immediately captivated me.

"I hope that you will be able to stay at the college to mix with the students," he said. I was told afterwards that certain friends "down east" had sent him one of my books, telling him to look out for me in case I arrived in Saskatoon, and it was to this letter that I owed the invitation.

The fellowship at the college was excellent. It was a pleasure to get to know the Principal, the Dean, and everybody. I made many contacts with the students, and finally they asked me to speak at their weekly service in the College chapel. I feel that it accomplished something.

The weather continued to be fairly cold. It snowed several times. One morning when I was out walking I was greatly interested in the beautiful hoar frost deposit on the naked trees—it made a scene to be gazed upon to be really appreciated. Snow, snow everywhere met the eye—the slightly undulating prairies becoming one great, white plain.

On Sunday morning, after Communion in the College chapel, I donned the cassock and surplice and gave the message of the Lord from the pulpit of St. James' Anglican Church. Dr. Haslam and another clergyman led the morning prayer. It was a simple and beautiful service. I have always appreciated the dignity and reverence of the Anglican services. During the afternoon, at the invitation of Professor Downer, I spoke to the Bible Class in Holy Trinity.

At seven o'clock it was my privilege to take the pulpit of the Cathedral of St. John's, Saskatoon. The Lord's presence was felt. The Dean had chosen the hymn, "Tell me the old, old story," to precede the sermon, and "Breathe on me, Breath of God," as a closing invocational hymn. From 8–30 p.m. it was my opportunity to address the Young People's Society in the Parish Hall.

The cathedral has a very interesting history. Away back in 1887, when there was not a single house or tree where Saskatoon now stands, the Anglican services were held in a tiny little school house in Nutana. At the beginning of the century the parish of St. John's was formed, growing rapidly, expanding its buildings, till, finally, the foundation stone of the present Cathedral was laid by H.R.H. the Duke of Connaught in 1912.

Many Anglicans are greatly interested in a spiritual awakening. Their type of Anglican Christianity is of the best, as is generally the case in Western Canada. The other denominations possess many potential channels for revival but one regrets to mention the prevalence of Liberalism among the United Church leaders. Many of these, however, are of the "old Methodist" evangelical type, and in them is the hope of revival in the great United Church of Canada.

Of the 922,000 people in Saskatchewan, the census indicates that 243,000 are United Church adherents, 234,000 Roman Catholics, 127,000 Anglicans, 55,000 Presbyterians, and 13,000 Baptists.

And so my visit to the prairie province of Saskatchewan came to an end. I left the spiritual results of the visit with the Lord. 'Twas He who arranged all things, and it is interesting to note that the two outstanding needs when I arrived were fully met—hospitality, which was provided lavishly, and 1 dollar 85 cents for a sleeper to Alberta—which reached me anonymously.

F

CHAPTER VIII

ALBERTA'S ROLLING PRAIRIES

THE Province of Alberta has a population of three-quarters of a million. It has much the same area as the other prairie provinces—a quarter of a million square miles: it has the same number of people to a square mile of territory as Manitoba—three, the other province, Saskatchewan, having four.

Edmonton and Calgary are the two principal cities. The former, with a population of 80,000, is the capital, situated in the northern part of Alberta, the latter, with 84,000, being a greater commercial centre situated in the south.

Like the inhabitants of the other prairie provinces, the Albertan thinks in terms of wheat. Wheatfields are everywhere, on a scale which would only bewilder a European farmer. Coal is worked in some places; in other districts there are oilwells. Alberta is certainly a province with a future.

I reached Edmonton at six o'clock in the morning. It was very cold, just as cold as it had been in Saskatoon, so my first thought was a warm breakfast. That attended to, I set off for the Post Office. The first man I met spoke with a slight accent, and as I am becoming an adept at guessing nationality, I said:

"Talar ni Svenska?"

"Ja," he replied in a very surprised way, and we

carried on quite a conversation. There are many Scandinavians, Germans and Galicians in Alberta.

Most of the morning I had spent in exploring the city and environs. While I was walking against the wind, my chin froze, giving me some funny sensations. But the dry cold is healthy, even if there are over forty degrees of frost. There is something exhilarating, and I enjoyed exercise in sub-zero temperatures.

At four o'clock in the afternoon, I found that I had not made any useful contacts. The thought came to me, "Why not introduce yourself to the Salvation Army officers?—they are always interested." The telephone book gave the name of the commanding officer, so I phoned through to his address. The Major was out, I was informed by the Major's wife, so that instead of talking to the Commanding Officer, I spoke to the Officer commanding the Commanding Officer. By five p.m. I had found my way over to the Citadel in Strathcona, where the Major was supposed to be.

It was really very amusing when I attempted to introduce myself. The muscles of my face had been partially frozen (unknown to me) and were beginning to thaw. My lips would not respond to everything that my nerves suggested, and I found myself talking with a sort of lisp. But the Major understood, knew my name, and soon there was quite a party of us down for supper. The Strathcona Corps was celebrating its anniversary of so many years' work, and the officers kindly invited me to take part in the programme.

I had another great pleasure in Edmonton. I telephoned the Secretary of the Premier, the Hon. William

Aberhart, Social Credit leader. The Secretary explained each time I phoned how busy the Premier was, but at last I got through to Mr. Aberhart himself. He was most courteous, told me how busy he was, suggested that as we were both taking part in the Army celebrations, the best arrangement was for both of us to come early to the church.

The eyes of the English-speaking world have been turned upon Alberta because of the Social Credit scheme which is being tried out there. I am not going to write of my own political sympathies; but, as a neutral observer, I feel that what I say regarding my happy contact with Mr. Aberhart will be of great interest to Christians everywhere.

From the platform, the Albertan Premier stated:

"And one of the reasons for my coming here is my sympathy for what you in the Army proclaim—firstly, Salvation through the merits of the shed Blood of Christ, which you and I and all of us know to be the only Way of Salvation: Secondly, Separation from the world and the things of the world, which is God's will for the believer."

Everyone who knows him, says that Mr. Aberhart is a sincere, upright Christian of the highest type. Calgary in the past has known the blessing which has followed his witness for Christ in the city. His radio Sunday School is one of the largest in the world.

"Of course, I believe in the Imminent Return of Our Lord," he told me. "That is the hope—the only hope of this world."

"Why I ask, Mr. Aberhart," said I, "is to have an answer for those Christians who think and say that your political work is just another ill-fated and misguided attempt to introduce millennial conditions instead of waiting for the King to come, whose right it is."

Mr. Aberhart looked at me keenly.

"You will remember, Mr. Orr, what one world-famous evangelist said when someone asked him what he would do if he *knew* that Christ would come to-morrow. He said simply 'I would go on with my work.'"

Mr. Aberhart, of course, believes that God has given him this political work to do. That is why so many follow him implicitly. But many readers will feel that therein lies the danger. That God would bless the sincere efforts of any Christian to uplift the conditions of life anywhere, I have not the shadow of a doubt. But I am not convinced that God will necessarily bless a certain definite scheme applied by a well-meaning man. The scheme may be contrary to God's will. I shall pray for Mr. Aberhart; I shall pray that God may bless Alberta through him: but until I am convinced that Social Credit is God's will for the people, I can have no liberty in praying for the success of this scheme, which promises to give twenty-five dollars' credit each month to everyone.

I think that it is the duty of every Christian reader to pray for Mr. Aberhart as a brother in Christ. Whether Social Credit is right or wrong should not alter such a responsibility. We have no idea of the dangers around the Premier. A militant group of Communists told a friend of mine that "we voted for Aberhart for our own

purposes." And their own purposes are to provoke a
crisis through the failure of Social Credit, and turn the
revulsion of feeling into revolutionary channels. Mr.
Aberhart has admittedly set himself a task, and it is one
of the most interesting experiments in history. No one
in Alberta doubts that the Premier is honestly doing his
utmost to keep his promises. I hate to read the slanders
of the Press elsewhere—that he is an adventurer. Two
minutes' talk with the Social Credit leader would con-
vince the sceptic of his crystal-clear earnestness and
uprightness.

Besides this pleasure of meeting the Premier, I had
the pleasure of being introduced by him to two members
of his Cabinet, both staunch Christians. It was a rare
treat to see a Cabinet Minister (the Hon. Mr. Fallow) lead
a Salvation Army Band, and it was another joy to hear
another Cabinet Minister (the Hon. Mr. Manning) say:

"I assure you that I often think in the midst of this
political work, there is no joy like the joy of preaching
the Gospel of Christ to the sinners who need it."

It was Mr. Manning who introduced me to the
audience.

During the time that the platform party was gathered
in the Pastor's vestry, the minister of the church arrived
and was introduced all round.

"Well," he said as he turned to me, "if you are really
Edwin Orr you must speak right now by telephone to a
friend of mine—a medical doctor who prays for you
every day."

The Doctor assured me that he remembered me
before the Throne of Grace every day for ever so long.

When I rang off, I said to Mr. Aberhart who was standing by:

"It is wonderful to have people praying like that."

"It is. I value it, too."

As the meeting was more in the nature of a celebration, I felt great scope for all that was Irish in me to express itself in an "after-dinner-speech." When those Albertans were told that Canada was the most wonderful country in the world, there was an appreciative murmur of applause. But when I added that Ireland was the most wonderful part of Canada, laughter and cheers rent the place. But even in such a meeting one can be faithful to the real message, so I began with fun, added narrative in a light vein, developed it into testimony to the power of our wonderful Saviour, and ended with a challenge.

Another strange thing happened in Edmonton. At supper table, one of the Army officers happened to mention that Dr. Philpott (the noted evangelist) was coming or had come to the city, and I interrupted with the words:

"Well, now, that's a man that I have been praying that I might meet. I've just missed him in several places."

We telephoned Dr. Philpott at the house of the pastor of Beulah Tabernacle, where he was to speak. Dr. Philpott had been praying about such a meeting too. Both he and Mr. Skitch (the pastor) had been down at Three Hills Bible College, where they had been praying that God would send me along: so leaving word at the college that, if I turned up in answer to prayer,

I was to be urged to visit Beulah Tabernacle in Edmonton, Mr. Skitch took the liberty of announcing to his flock that they were not to be surprised if a young Irishman came before the week was out.

Consequently, Dr. Philpott urged me to come to his meeting after the Army one. I got into a taxi, arrived at 9.20 p.m., and we started all over again. Wasn't I glad that I went. The atmosphere of the place was charged with the expectancy of revival, and there was a great breaking down in the after-meeting which remained full. I was greatly surprised and not a little heartened to hear several burst into beautiful prayers in Norwegian, Swedish and German.

At midnight, the train left Edmonton for Calgary. I reached Calgary next morning at eight o'clock. The usual routine began again—just as it begins in every place where I have no friends—breakfast, Post Office, exercise. At ten o'clock I called on a Presbyterian minister of whom I had heard. He did not know me at first, but soon he was a fast friend and was extending the hospitality of his home. At noon we arranged a luncheon for six friends, and this was very satisfactorily engaged in at a down-town restaurant. It is one of my greatest delights to meet strangers who have been remembering my work in prayer.

"I met a commercial traveller the other day," said one friend, "and he asked me 'Have you seen that fellow Orr in these parts?' I told him that I had not, whereupon he told me of something that will interest you, Mr. Orr."

This commercial traveller, a Christian, had engaged a coloured porter in conversation in the train, had lent him "Can God?" which was used of God to the porter's conversion.

"And so that is how I knew that you were coming this way."

Another young man had heard from my friends in Brandon, and so on. What a delight to arrive in a city without a friend, and within four hours to discover a colony of friends.

The first meeting was arranged in the Gospel Mission, the people being notified by telephone the same day. Then a little paragraph was put into a local paper, announcing that a meeting would be held in the Presbyterian Church on the Wednesday evening. This was well-filled and there was evidence of the Lord's presence with us.

I was much surprised to find the weather conditions in Calgary so mild compared with those of other cities around. This is due to the Chinook, a wind which sometimes blows through the gap in the mountains, bringing the warmth of the Pacific with it. Sometimes in Calgary there has been a temperature of 20 degrees below zero, and two hours later a temperature of 30 above—this amazing rise of fifty degrees being due to the Chinook. An arch of clouds heralds the coming of the Chinook. Then the Calgary observer may phone up a friend in Banff—many miles west—and learn the good news, "Yes, it's getting warmer here."

There is an old story told—it should not be repeated to Calgary people who have heard it so often—of a man who described a gallop down the trail from Banff to Calgary. He was driving a pair of horses attached to a sleigh. They stopped at a house; the thermometer stood many degrees below zero. But coming out of the house, the man felt the warm westerly breeze, and knew that if the snow melted he would not get home on the sleigh. So he whipped up the horses, drove with the wind (literally) and told his friends in Calgary, that "all the way the front part of the steel runners on the sleigh were on icy snow, while the back part was in water."

One often hears folks warn a youthful speaker "not to become swelled-headed." This sad state was actually the case with me one day in Calgary. The minister, his daughter, and I set off for the Banff trail together. I had expressed a desire to learn to *ski*. With the minister's daughter as instructor, and the minister as an amused spectator, I began to pick up the whole idea as quickly as one could do so. The first time or so I lost my balance, but afterwards my success made me desirous of better sport. We went over the hills together, looking for steeper and steeper slopes after each attempt. At last I found a great run, and commenced the speedy descent, my instructor watching me from the top of the hill. Towards the bottom, I struck a bad patch, and fell headlong. It was providential that my eye was not put out by the point of the *ski*. As things were, I had such a swelled head that I could not wear my hat for several days.

I have already mentioned the Prairie Bible College at Three Hills, and the fact that some folks there were praying about my visit. My real problem was the absence of suitable transport, but at last the Rev. Mr.

Rodgers told me that he would motor me out. Accompanied by a graduate student, we set out. I was greatly impressed by all that I saw. The Prairie Bible Institute was commenced just a short time ago by a young minister named Maxwell. The story sounds like a page from the story of George Müller or the China Inland Mission. No debts were incurred, and yet building after building went up, till this year there are 250 students in residence. This wonderful school supplies men and women to the C.I.M. and other well known societies.

We arrived in time for lunch, after which I had the pleasure of addressing the school. After supper, we had a wonderful time. I felt great liberty in speaking, spoke for two hours, and then witnessed the power of God in the after-meeting. It was wonderful to hear those students pray for individual revival, confess all sort of hindrances, and return thanks for blessing received.

The Prairie Bible Institute at Three Hills will do much for the work of God in Alberta and all through Canada. Its witness has already done much to magnify the name of Christ. Three Hills is a prime factor in the hope of revival in the Dominion—such is the opinion of many of my friends.

Alberta has much the same needs as the other parts of Canada. There is the same indifference: the same spiritual drowsiness prevails; and yet there are little groups of intercessors for revival. The United Church is the strongest body numerically, followed by the Roman Catholics, the Anglicans, the Presbyterians and the

Baptists. Among those who are earnestly seeking revival
there is a certain amount of unity, but not the degree
that one would hope for. Too often there is the desire
for denominational revival, a selfish desire which has
no fulfilment. It is when we want to see the Body of
Christ receive a time of refreshing from the presence
of the Lord that our hopes have a prospect of fulfilment.

It has not been possible to keep a diary this year,
and so my memory has had to serve substitute. During
this Canadian trip, I have had to adopt a more systematic
plan than heretofore. Each week I have dispatched
a section of my manuscript to my publishers, and as
this has been typed during long train journeys, the
manuscript has taken the place of a diary.

As I work at it now, we are approaching one of the
scenic wonders of the world—the Rocky Mountains.
The Albertan foothills are themselves very pretty, but
now we are getting closer and closer to the mountains
themselves. Just now the Canadian Pacific train has
passed a frozen lake, which in summer would be a
sapphire gem set about with emerald. Half the sky
is now taken up by the splendid mountain giants. At
the bottom, are beautiful trees of every variety possible;
the middle slopes are pine-clad; and the peaks themselves are a beautiful study in black and white. One
is forcibly reminded of Switzerland.

The railroad is now running parallel with a pretty
river—as yet unfrozen. The valley has widened again,
but still the background is formed by the grandeur
of those mighty peaks. There is one, for all the world

like a mighty fist raised in defiance to the sky by Mother
Earth; here a twin peak resembling the heavy head of
a steer: there a lonely sentinel, watching, watching.
The whole range looks like a huge wall of rock, a great
impassable barrier. Long shadows are becoming
shorter as the brilliant sun is rising into the sky of azure
blue. What a grand picture. From my own small
window I can count twenty snow-capped peaks;
here in the foreground are some leafless trees; beyond
are the dark green coniferous forests: and once more the
eye travels upward to the jagged peaks thrust into the
dome of blue.

The scene has changed again. Another wall crowned
by another dozen mountain giants fills the view. The
vista is an everchanging one—new wonders being
brought to view each moment. Now we are passing
closer to a great castle of rock, whose battlements,
snow-crowned, frown down upon the creeping humans
in the valley below. The mountain wears an air of
indifference as the train travels onward into the heart
of the range.

The Bow River, whose course the railroad follows,
is now frozen over. The temperature has dropped
many degrees, and will continue to drop as the train
ascends the gradient to the great divide.

I greatly enjoyed the short time spent at Banff, the
popular mountain resort. Banff is beautifully situated
—from the station there is a magnificent panorama to
be seen. The great bulk of Cascade Mountain (9,836
feet) fills the view to the north, towering over the town.
To the east is the Fairholme Range. Up the valley to

the west are the snowy peaks of the range above the Simpson Pass. Banff is eighty miles from Calgary, and the elevation of the railroad is 4,500 feet.

The average reader will scarcely be able to grasp the idea of the tremendous size of the Canadian Rockies. I have already compared them to the Swiss Alps, but the comparison is futile. Edward Whymper, the hero of the Matterhorn, described the Canadian Rockies as fifty Switzerlands in one—and this is certainly no exaggeration. It takes an express train five hours to cross the Alps from Lucerne to Como. The train on which I crossed the Rockies—"the Dominion," the fastest C.P.R. express—takes 23 hours to cross the mountains from Cochrane to Mission on the other side. There is 600 miles of glorious Alpine scenery—and of course the Rockies are longer north and south than east and west.

Leaving Banff, we are following the Bow River towards its source. The train goes slowly, for we are rising all the time. Here Castle Mountain is a huge precipice of over 4,000 feet sheer drop—its name being given on account of its resemblance to an old castle. Now we catch a glimpse of the magnificent Storm Mountain, and not far away the snowy dome of Mount Ball. The scenery is becoming more and more beautiful.

The train is now approaching the famous Lake Louise, one of the most beautiful lakes in the world. The peaks that surround it form a circle of beauty seldom surpassed. The Great Artist hangs here a masterpiece, indeed the masterpiece of the art gallery of the Rockies. It is a treat to be able to travel through these wonderful mountains. The author, always ambitious for travelling but always handicapped in the matter of finance, can thankfully say, "He shall give thee the desires of thine heart."

Six miles west of Lake Louise is the Great Divide, 5,300 feet. This is the highest elevation of the Canadian Pacific Railway. On one side is the word Alberta: on the other British Columbia. The Great Divide is the watershed of the continent. The waters which flow east join the Bow River which flows into the South Saskatchewan, which in turn finds its way into Lake Winnipeg and thence to Hudson Bay and the Atlantic. The waters flowing west into the Kicking Horse River make their way through the great Columbia River to the Pacific Ocean.

Ahead of us, as we leave Alberta, is a wall of cloud. Some of the mountains behind exceed 11,000 feet in elevation. It was well worth while coming—so with that thought I'll say Good-bye, Alberta.

CHAPTER IX

BEAUTIFUL BRITISH COLUMBIA

THE Kicking Horse pass was our gateway to British Columbia. There seemed to be more fresh snow on the slopes as we passed, no doubt due to the westerly winds which deposit their moisture on the slopes. The mountains around were hidden by the heavy, white blanket of mist which hid from our view such giants as Waputik (8,977), Niblock (9,764) and Daly (10,342). The gradient during the past twenty miles has been very difficult, three locomotives being required to pull the train up to the highest point, and two being used to keep it from running away as we go down hill.

We are just about to enter the famous spiral tunnels —6,000 feet long—one of the marvels of railroad engineering. Formerly the section between the Great Divide and Field had an exceptionally difficult gradient. But now the gradient is much reduced, due to one of the greatest engineering feats in history. From the east, the train enters the first tunnel under Cathedral Mountain, and turns an almost complete circle inside the mountain. As we went round I could feel the centrifugal force. The tunnel passes under itself, and emerges into daylight forty-eight feet lower.

The second part of the tunnel enters Ogden Mountain, again turns right round, passes under itself, the train emerging into light at a level forty-five feet lower. This wonderful tunnel is a perfect maze, the railway doubling back on itself twice, and forming a rough figure of 8. We are now arriving at the town of Field, above which towers Mount Stephan, 10,495 feet. At Field, we change from Mountain Time to Pacific Time, putting watches an hour back. Pacific time is five hours behind Atlantic time used in Halifax—one example of the huge distance across the Continent.

Westwards from Field, the railroad descends steeply, still following the Kicking Horse River Canyon until Golden is reached. Then we go alongside the great Columbia River (1,400 miles long): through the Connaught Tunnel (five miles long): over the Selkirk Range, downhill again to Salmon Arm.

.   .   .   .   .

At Salmon Arm there came one of those little incidents which prove the providence of God in little things. Whilst in Toronto, I received a little note from a young man in service for God in the Okanagan Valley, in which is situated Salmon Arm, Armstrong, Vernon, and other little towns of about 500 inhabitants. He suggested that I should step off if possible for a few meetings in the Valley, a suggestion which (humanly speaking) I could not for one moment consider, when at that time I was being compelled to refuse invitations to speak in large centres and big cities in other more important areas. I prayed about it, and felt that I should accept the invitation despite the apparent folly of arranging to speak to a group of 40 when I could be addressing as many hundreds.

G

Consequently I wrote to the young preacher and his associate, telling them to expect me on a certain Saturday morning at 10.51 a.m. In the meantime, the pastor, his family, and his associate (my correspondent, whom I had met in Wales) moved down the valley to reside in Armstrong. I wrote a second letter suggesting that they should try to meet the 9 p.m. Friday train instead. By a strange coincidence both men were up at Salmon Arm that day. The Post Office had forwarded the mail to the new address in Armstrong, thirty miles away, but had kept *my* letter in Salmon Arm—otherwise my train would not have been met.

We motored up the rough and stony road to Armstrong, and after a night's rest, we had our first meeting. The people came from great distances to attend the meeting in the little chapel; and the second meeting was of the same order, but was held in Salmon Arm. Without consulting me, the pastor announced a thanks-offering. As the people are very poor, the offering was proportionately tiny. I could see that the dear fellow, the pastor, looking very worried, was coming to apologise for the smallness of the gift. I interrupted him to give him something for his fine work in the Valley.

"Oh, no, Brother, I cannot take this. *We* owe *you* a debt, not you *us*."

"If I had come for money," said I, "I wouldn't have stepped off at a tiny little place like this. I came to share in your work, so take this for it, and don't attempt to refuse what the good Lord sends you."

Tears came into his eyes.

"I had not meant to tell you, Brother. We had run out of both gasoline and the price of it. God has answered my prayer in a most unexpected way."

My hearts bleeds for the pastors of such little bethels in out-of-the-way places. They have suffered a great shrinkage of income, have tightened their belts and said nothing, nobly carrying on a magnificent effort to make Christ known in places unheard-of.

In one such place where I happened to ask questions, I was told that, for one hundred miles in any direction, there was not another witness for the Gospel of free Grace. The need of the "Wild West" is a pressing one. The Chief Scout, Lord Baden-Powell, has said of the Canadian parson "his parish is a large, unsettled district of 5,000 square miles in which he has four or five small churches. The roads are nothing more than logging trails in most places. He could go home and have a nice little parish of his own with not much to do . . . but he prefers to stay where he is and do what he calls *his job*. That is the class of missionary to whom I take off my hat as being a true member of the Ancient Order of Tough Nuts."

At 9 p.m. the Canadian Pacific "Dominion" steamed into the little station of Salmon Arm, and for five minutes the little snow-covered place became a hive of activity. At last the heavy train began to pull out of the station. I waved my farewell to my new friends, and went to the sleeping wagon—so to sleep.

Next morning, when I awoke, we were already getting near Vancouver. Upon arrival, I kept a look-out for

Rev. W. Arnold Bennett, an Old Country friend who had heard of my coming and who had arranged a programme in advance. Mr. Bennett's ministry in Belfast had been used of God for the spiritual deepening of my own life, so I was quite eager to renew the contact which had been broken by our last parting in Whitley Bay, Northumberland. On the platform I caught sight of his familiar figure. Soon we were talking, and he introduced another gentleman who became the kindest of hosts during my stay. His lovely home became my home *pro tem*, and his "helpmeet" looked after me splendidly.

Mr. Bennett handed me a printed advertisement card, which stated:

Meetings as follows:

Sunday,   November 24, 11 a.m.   Broadway West Baptist Church.
Sunday,   November 24, 7.30 p.m.   ,,
Sunday,   November 24, 3 p.m.   Christian Institute.
Monday,   November 25, 10 a.m.   Ministers' and Leaders' Conference.
Monday,   November 25, 8 p.m.   First Baptist Church, N. Vancouver.
Tuesday,   November 26, 8 p.m.   Ruth Morton Baptist Church.
Wednesday, November 27, 8 p.m.   Metropolitan Tabernacle.
Thursday,   November 28, 8 p.m.   United Church, W. Vancouver.
Friday,   November 29, 8 p.m.   Christian Institute.
Saturday,   November 30, 8 p.m.   Special Rally, including Inter-School Christian Fellowship; Varsity Christian Union; Young People's Groups of Gr. Vancouver.
Afternoon meetings at 3 o'clock—Tuesday, Wednesday, Thursday in the Christian Institute.

"You have filled the week up well," said I.

Mr. Bennett laughed.

"And I had to put others off as well."

Before the week actually finished, I found that there were three meetings a day—eighteen in all.

"Mr. Bennett, Mr. Bennett, will you tell me when I am going to write three chapters of my book? And what about my letters?"

"Well, Brother, you must take things easy. . . ."

Thank God for all the fellowship and fraternity extended by Rev. Arnold Bennett. He fulfilled all my great expectations . . . as organiser, director, guide, philosopher and friend. The meetings were well planned, beginning in the suburbs and then converging on the city. From the commencement there was blessing.

At Kitsilano, where Broadway West (Mr. Bennett's) Church is situated, we hired the Alma Academy for the Sunday services. At night it was found necessary to bring in extra chairs, and even then there were folks looking for room. At the end of the address, there was a time of prayer and an immediate response to the appeal for those seeking revival, restoration, or salvation. After the first named had been dealt with, Mr. Bennett very wisely asked the "backsliders" and "sinners" to remain behind, dealt with them, and reported that there were genuine decisions for Christ among the dozen who stayed.[1]

[1]*An Appreciation of the ministry of J. Edwin Orr, by Rev. W. Arnold Bennett, Vancouver, B.C.*

Among Vancouver Christians there has been much mutual expression of desire for Revival, and sincere longing of heart for a move-

Rev. Andrew Grieve wrote in describing the meeting in his church (Ruth Morton): "From there he led his audience to the Cross of Christ. . . . The hush of the Holy Spirit was upon the meeting, and God was working in the hearts of His people. Then came the invitation (without any unnecessary persuasion) to which many responded. We sang softly the invocation: 'I need Thee every hour' while confessing the need of personal heart-revival. One man who signified his return to the Lord told me that his decision was the climax of the Lord's dealings with him throughout the week. We bless God for the meeting, believing it to be a step nearer the realisation of the answer to our prayers for a widespread spiritual revival in the Church of Christ."

In North Vancouver there were many signs of blessing. And in West Vancouver, the appeal was not without many responses. I had the privilege of preaching the

---

ment of God has characterised a great number. Because of this the visit of Mr. J. Edwin Orr has been keenly welcomed. There is no doubt whatever that Mr. Orr has been called of God to the ministry of Prayer for Revival, and is being used of the Lord to stir a sleeping church everywhere to a sense of responsibility and to a realisation of what God is able to do when His people pray. Our brother has a message which the people are willing to listen to, and which refreshes the souls of believers. Mr. Orr's ministry in Vancouver and district has been a gracious one, very encouraging audiences have gathered and God has blessed His Word to the revival of many believers and also to the salvation of souls. There is a feeling amongst us that this visit will ripen the already existing desire for Revival in these parts and bring together a host of God's people for prayer and revival effort. Mr. Orr has made a strong appeal to the young people, and it is from these ranks that we have the greatest hopes of a movement of God that shall sweep this great North-west country and bring revival blessing to the whole of the needy Dominion of Canada. May the Lord keep our Brother Edwin Orr, and abundantly use him in this wonderful ministry of mobilising prayer force for mighty revival the world over.

W. Arnold Bennett.

Word in the Girls' Corner Club, stressing the need of personal revival to the young ladies assembled. There were decisions of unconverted girls at the close.

In the great Metropolitan Tabernacle (pastor, Rev. W. M. Robertson) the subject chosen dealt with Russia, where I took the liberty of correcting a few wrong impressions given by a local minister of liberal views. In this meeting, as at the University meeting, there were present some people of Communistic leanings. But in the Tabernacle, the police guard was not needed, the people listening attentively. The address was broadcast. I had one apprehension during the meeting —for a woman suddenly got up, walked down the aisle, ascended the choir steps, and came towards me. I hesitated a moment to think a way of guarding the microphone, but was greatly relieved to find that the lady was a deaf person trying to hear.

The afternoon meetings continued to be well attended. The first Bible reading was from the Epistle to the Romans on Full Surrender; the second from the Acts of the Apostles on the Filling of the Spirit; and the third and last on the secret of Abiding in Christ. Various people told me of the suitability of the message to their needs. The Word is always applicable.

After the address one evening in the Christian Institute, a lady came to me and said:

"May I have a word with you?"

"Certainly. Sit down a moment and I'll be free as soon as I shake hands with these people."

As soon as I was free, I sat down beside the lady, who apparently was in her "fifties," and who seemed to be "comfortably off." I had used the verse "In Thy presence is fulness of joy." So I said:

"You don't appear to be happy. What's the trouble?"

"If it was not for the fear of Hell, I would commit suicide. Oh, I am so miserable."

She restrained her tears.

"Do you think that it is God's Will for you to be like this?" I asked.

She told me a story of disobedience and backsliding. I listened, knowing well that she needed to unburden her heart. Apparently she had once experienced the joy of salvation, but was now in the depths of despair, not knowing the assurance of faith.

We knelt for prayer, and I urged her to confess her backsliding to God. This she was very ready to do. Her misery found expression in her prayer.

"Now," said I. "You have asked God to forgive you. It is your duty to thank Him for hearing and answering your prayer."

And so an unhappy soul found peace.

At the United Church in West Vancouver, the meeting was arranged by the Women's Evangelistic Band. The Lord used Miss Frances Brook, joined afterwards by her sisters, to begin this much-blessed work. The Peace River District, between Alberta and British Columbia, was the first field to be worked by these courageous women. The little band began to grow in strength. West Vancouver became the headquarters of the W.E.B. (and there I had supper, for Miss Brook is an aunt of my friend Raymond Joyce in faraway Central Asia.) The work is still growing and God is blessing. These ladies are full of interest in revival, and I am sure that the Lord is already using them as channels of revival.

I am not likely to forget the Young People's Rally on the Saturday night. The great majority of the audience was composed of young men and women whose ages varied from fifteen to thirty. The young people of to-day are intensely honest, and one can truthfully say that they are not a bit sophisticated. The response to the message surprised me. Many young men walked right up to the front to confess that from then on, Christ would be Lord as well as Saviour. There were scores of girls, not a few in tears. The appeal was not an emotional one, indeed one could say that emotion was non-existent in the appeal. I heard afterwards that Saturday night was a climax in the experience, step by step, of many young Christians. My heart rejoiced—knowing what a help a similar opportunity of public witness had been to me. Christians ought not to forget that God has entrusted His work to youth, unspoiled, earnest, honest youth. How many older Christians there are who confess that they missed God's call while young, and that they have lived in regrets ever since.

Thank God, there were also decisions to accept Christ as Saviour, for whenever He is magnified by His own, others are attracted to Him. I left the meeting very tired and very happy.

I arrived in the city of Victoria next morning. A kind friend called at the ship, coming down to the cabin to tell me that he would take me to my headquarters. I was *tired*. I told him to wait a couple of minutes. I felt dazed by sleepiness, went to sleep again.

The programme in Victoria was very full. Beginning in St. Paul's Presbyterian Church, and continuing in the Central Baptist Church, the meetings were well attended by people of all denominations. I noticed a letter signed by a retired C.I.M. missionary (Dr. Julius Hewett) published by the *Daily Colonist*. It drew the attention of readers to the visit and quoted one of Rev. Oswald Smith's reports in *The Christian*. This, together with other advertisements, brought crowds to the meetings, so that the accommodation was taxed to the limit.

I do not like "writing up" meetings at which I have taken a part, but I feel, nevertheless, that my prayer partners desire to learn details of how the Lord answers their prayers. Here is Rev. J. B. Rowell's report:

J. Edwin Orr in the most English City outside England —Victoria, British Columbia

"Many of the Christian people of Victoria had already read the fascinating books of Mr. Orr, and many had prayed that the Lord would send blessing through the visit of His servant, deepening the spiritual life of God's people, reclaiming those walking at a distance from their Lord, and winning the unsaved for Christ.

"On Sunday December the First, 1935, Mr. Orr arrived. It was evident from one glance at him, that he had been working to the limit. However, he had poured himself out in the Lord's service, and we realised that he had not come to Victoria alone, but that the Holy Spirit was still his Strength and Stay.

"During the first day, Sunday, he spoke seven times. From the first it was clear that one desire was uppermost—to tell of Christ as the Living, Bright Reality. The Presence of the Holy Spirit was realised in many hearts, and that night a number publicly expressed their desire to know Christ as personal Saviour. Mr. Orr also broadcast two messages over the radio from station C.F.C.T., and words of appreciation from the ' shut-in' were received next day."

On the way up from the Radio Station to the Church, I stopped at a Salvation Army Open Air Meeting. The local officer was walking round the fringe of the crowd on the side-walk, giving a friendly word of greeting to each person.

"How are you getting on here?" I asked.

"Splendidly," replied the officer. "You have come some distance?"

"Ireland," I answered.

"That's a long way. Is it business that brings you here?"

"The King's Business."

I gave him the little advertisement slip.

"Well, well, well. Shake hands again. I have been praying for you."

At his request, I spoke in the ring, and we had a fine time together. The Salvation Army, as well as other places, gave up their Monday meeting and came along to the Monday Evening Rally, which was utterly packed out. It was a Young People's Meeting, hundreds of fine young men and women crowding the church. I sang for them in French, Norwegian, German and Portuguese. Getting into my stride, I adapted myself to the young folk, ignoring the older ones entirely. They soon were laughing at the amusing incidents of travels, marvelling at God's goodness, and all the while being prepared for the serious issues of the address. When the challenge came, scores and scores responded, coming up to the platform to confess a dedication of life and service. There were also decisions to accept Christ. At 10.30 p.m. I had finished dealing with the last enquirer (a man who accepted Christ as Saviour) and so finished the visit to Victoria. I caught the midnight steamer to Vancouver. And now as I type this, I am getting ready for my "Farewell to Canada" meeting in Mount Pleasant Church.

British Columbia has a population of three-quarters of a million, of whom two-fifths (or 300,000) reside in Greater Vancouver. The Province is vast, possessing 360,000 square miles of territory, and, as a consequence, the population is very scattered—two persons for each square mile. The country is very mountainous and very beautiful, and it is invaded by thousands upon thousands of tourists every year. The country is divided into three—the Coast Range, the Plateau, and the Rockies. At the coast, the climate is very moderate —just like that of England, including November fogs. Here there is abundant moisture and sunshine, causing the trees to grow to great heights. I have been inside a hollow tree *in an automobile.* The plateau and mountain areas have a Continental climate like the other parts of Canada.

Vancouver City has grown phenomenally in recent years. The ever-increasing trade of the Pacific has created competition between the four great Pacific ports—Los Angeles, San Francisco, Seattle and Vancouver. The Canadian city has many advantages over its rivals, and promises to become a great Pacific metropolis. Vancouver is the terminus of the two great Trans-Canada railways, the gateway to the Orient, a centre of industry, and as such, its future is assured.

Evangelical witness in the city is not increasing proportionately. There are many dead, liberal churches, carrying on with a "social club" programme, and ignoring the prime business of a church—soul-winning. The Evangelicals themselves are very dis-united. Some are doing a fine work in a limited circle—but there is a great lack of co-ordination of effort.

A Christian gentleman, who is interested in children's work, told me that many Vancouver children had never heard the name of Jesus.

"No, sir," said one growing girl, "I never heard of *Him*. Who is He, please?"

And what is true of Vancouver, is all the more true of other parts. Victoria, the capital—a city of 40,000 situated on Vancouver Island which is twice the size of Wales—is a very sleepy place,[1] especially spiritually. Lethargy has seized hold of most of the churches,

---

[1] A lady resident of Victoria is now in hospital, having yawned for over nine weeks. Personally, I felt that way myself in Victoria.

so much so, that the few live places are crying out in despair.

British Columbia is seven times the size of England, but England has forty times the population of the Farther West Province of Canada. It takes imagination to visualise a province 750 miles long and 450 miles wide. British Columbia possessed vast, untold, untapped wealth—minerals, timber, fish, etc. The population is bound to grow, and truly one can say that B.C. has the rosiest prospects of all Canada.

Spiritually? The outlook is full of difficulties, but many are hoping for a revival, knowing it to be their only hope. The future lies in the hands of these few who pray for revival. If they pray and then receive revival, the blessing will spread all over the Province.

CHAPTER X

THE DOMINION OF YOUTH AND OPPORTUNITY

CANADA is one of the most wonderful countries in the world. It is a new country—almost entirely new. One can truthfully describe the Dominion of Canada as a land of Youth and Opportunity. The latent wealth of the Dominion is tremendous and the fringe of it has scarcely even been touched.

Canada is a sub-continent, in area as big as Europe. I laugh when I think of the funny ideas held by my British friends. They say: "Don't forget when you get to Montreal to look up my cousin Jimmy in Winnipeg." They do not seem to realize that the distance between these two cities is about *four times* that between London and Edinburgh. It takes a week of constant train travel to get from coast to coast. Canada would comfortably hold six hundred Englands. These facts give just a little idea of Canada's vast size.

The population of Canada is only ten million. In racial origin, five and a half million of these are of British stock. Half a million Germans and two hundred Scandinavians are rapidly becoming Anglicised. Then there are three million French, mostly Roman Catholic and increasing as Roman Catholics do by the large family policy. There are also 200,000 Ukrainians, and smaller bodies of immigrants from other countries.

The American Indians are few and far between. All this conglomeration of nationality is in the melting pot, the crucible which will produce the New Canadian. With the exception of the French, whose religion and language tend to keep them separate, Canadians are being welded together to become a greater Britain beyond the seas. Both native and immigrant are intensely loyal to the land which supports them, and the population could easily grow to eighty millions, for Canada has enough land and natural wealth to support ten times her population. The Canadian people have definite characteristics—they are wonderfully open-hearted, very generous, tremendously honest. There is much to attract a student and the Canadian temperament is quite a study in itself.

Canada has not yet developed a culture of her own, and yet one could not say that she is a copyist of any other country. Canada thinks as Britain does, and lives as the Americans do. By studying her great southern neighbour, the great Dominion has avoided many pitfalls, and yet has benefitted by the progress of the U.S.A. The influence of Great Britain has had a very steadying effect in Canadian life. But Canada is— just Canada. One cannot compare her with any other nation for such comparisons are odious.

A factor in the spiritual life of the Dominion—and a disturbing factor at that—is the materialism of Canadians generally. Most immigrants arrived in Canada with the ambition of "getting on" financially, and this great ambition absorbs everything. Such an ambition is a great asset in the material progress and development of the country, but it is an equally great hindrance to cultural and spiritual growth. "Man shall not live by bread alone—" The tragedy of Canada is that too many Canadians are so busy "getting on" and laying up treasure on earth that they have not a moment to spare in considering their welfare in the life to come.

And so *materialism* is a menace in Canada. With this materialism is its twin brother—rationalism in religion. Most of the colleges of Canada have compromised with this cancerous growth, and in consequence, their products are generally liberal thinkers who preach a social gospel. That these liberals are in earnest, I have not the shadow of a doubt. But their advent has caused paralysis in the professing church in the Dominion.

I spoke one night on *Where are the dead?* My audience, I think, expected me to deal with the question of the future state. They were greatly surprised. Declaring that 90 per cent of the dead were in the churches, I gave them quite a few facts to think over. There are big dead churches everywhere and to them the Lord's injunction certainly applies. "Because thou sayest, I am rich and increased with goods, and have need of nothing; and knowest not that thou art wretched, and miserable, and poor, and blind, and naked; I counsel thee to buy of Me gold tried in the fire—"

One tragedy in Canada is the death of prayer meetings and evangelistic work. In some of the cities such as Toronto and Winnipeg, there is any amount of evangelistic work but in others such work is entirely unknown.

H

Many parts of the Maritime provinces are poverty-stricken in spiritual things, a sort of formalism being the rule in church worship. Strange to say the people are often loyal to these dead institutional churches—why I cannot say, unless it be that they must have some centre of loyalty, and so the church has become a club. In Quebec Province, Roman Catholicism holds sway. Almost every Christian Canadian would describe Montreal as a very wicked city. Moving westward to Ontario, even here we find liberalism entrenched and the evangelicals bickering among themselves. What I have said of the North of England towns, I will repeat regarding the Prairie towns in Manitoba, Saskatchewan and Alberta. In these towns one may find one live church, two half-alive, three dead and the remainder breathing very heavily. Lethargy seems to have seized hold on the professing Christians. They don't seem to have known any better and so they have nothing to aim at. Smug complacency is the rule. In British Columbia, there are huge areas without a true gospel witness.

Ireland, Wales, Korea, United States and many countries have experienced gracious visitations of the Spirit. So many Christians have been revived in such experiences that we can call these visitations "National Revivals." Canadian Christians must never forget that there has never been a Canadian National Revival. Why is this? Some Christians have given one reason; others have given me another reason, but my reply has always been the same. Circumstances are nothing: temperaments are nothing: occupations are nothing—

fulfil the conditions and you get the results. Canada needs a revival, and needs it badly. There is not a sign of a revival in the horizon, except *one*.

East, West, North, South, I have found little groups of intercessors whose hearts God has touched. The burden of their prayer is,"Lord, send a revival to Canada, and begin now in me."

If, as I believe, revival actually begins in prayer, then the revival in Canada has begun. God does not put prayer for revival into the hearts of Canadian peoples to mock them. The prayer itself is of God and as such is sure of an answer just as soon as God is permitted to work.

Every Canadian Christian who has studied the matter, agrees that there is undoubtedly a fellowship of prayer for revival. What can we do to deepen it. The best work of deepening is by stimulating, intensifying, mobilizing and directing *prayer*. I have every hope of this being done. The conference of ministers in Toronto were unanimous in agreeing that some steps should be taken to deepen the sense of revival fellowship throughout the country. Already steps have been taken to arrange that prayer requests from Christians of every province will be circulated among the praying people in prayer groups.

Take for instance the position in British Columbia. I have just come from the third little conference of Vancouver ministers and leaders interested in revival. Several gratifying facts are worthy of notice. First of all these ministers and leaders take the attitude of "revival at any cost." Secondly, unknown to many of us, a prayer union for revival had just begun in Vancouver, its leaders knowing little about our work, using exactly the same terminology, and now not only willing but eager to work with us in mobilizing prayer for British Columbia in fullest co-operation with a Dominion-wide effort. It was interesting to hear other points raised. The need of a British Columbian "Keswick" was stressed, it being hoped that something could be done in conjunction with the Canadian Keswick at Muskoka in Ontario. Muskoka is 3,000 miles away from parts of British Columbia. Then it was also suggested that the outcome of this prayer fellowship might be a much needed united evangelistic campaign in Vancouver. Finally, the delegates agreed that they would adopt the programme of mobilization of prayer, leaving all other issues to be dealt with when the time became ripe.

What these British Columbians suggest doing in their province can be done in every province. I am very hopeful of seeing a prayer bulletin for revival in Canada being published in Toronto circulated throughout the Dominion and compiled with prayer requests from leaders in every province. Any Canadian reader who feels interested could write to Rev. Oswald Smith until such time as an editor is appointed.

That God will answer prayer I have not the shadow of a doubt. Prayer brings confession of sin, confession requires cleansing, cleansing permits the Holy Spirit to work, the Holy Spirit is the author and hope of revival.

And what of the individual? Revival in Canada

will begin when individuals seek individual blessing. The reader of this knows his need. He knows also that God can supply all his needs. Why not ask God to do it now? The individual will thus possess a personal revival which passed on will lead to wide-spread blessing. That is the way revival comes.

I am grateful to God that I can report having seen times of refreshing from the presence of the Lord. The more one sees, the more one is eager for a greater one; and at this moment my prayer for Canada is one with that of thousands of Canadians—we seek times of refreshing from the presence of the Lord.

CHAPTER XI

THE PRESENCE OF THE LORD

"REPENT ye therefore, and be converted, that your sins may be blotted out, when times of refreshing shall come from the presence of the Lord."

This great statement of the Apostle Peter shows clearly that the source of revival is the presence of the Lord.

"Times of refreshing from the presence of the Lord." The thought surely opens up for us a mental vista of the possibilities of blessing through seeking God's presence—possibilities often hidden by the thick clouds of our own great ignorance. To be in the presence of the Lord is to be revived. When a community of believers is brought low before the presence of the Lord—when the very air that they breathe appears to be supercharged with the sense of His presence—that is the beginning of revival. It *is* revival.

What has Scripture to say about the presence of the Lord? The study of such teaching makes us all the more anxious for the blessing of His presence.

"Glory and honour are in His presence: strength and gladness are in His place."[1] Are such worth having? Would we rather keep the shame, the dishonour, the weakness, the misery that is ours away from His presence?

[1] Corinthians, 16, 27.

Every Ulsterman can explain to the reader what a "Lurgan spade" is. It is a big long, mournful-looking spade, and it gives rise to the expression, "a face like a Lurgan spade." I am sorry to say that many Christians have the bad reputation of having a face like a Lurgan spade. The world consequently thinks that religion is a "Kill-joy." Why do Christians look so sad? It cannot be that they are burdened by the needs of the masses—their conduct generally forbids such an explanation. I met one such sorrowful one and I said:

"Cheer up. In His presence is fulness of joy. If you are not happy, you know how to be. Get into the presence of the Lord."

In His presence is fulness of joy. Herein lies the antidote to all our worries, the remedy for all our big sighs, the panacea for all perplexities. There is no need to fret. The Christian who is worrying is out of touch with God. If the reader who reads these words is worrying, let me say, "You need a time of refreshing from the presence of the Lord."

I have witnessed many revivals of God's people—both individuals and companies. The Holy Spirit's working always brought a fulness of joy. Cups ran over. Worries disappeared. When Love, and Joy, and Peace came in at the door, Misery went up the chimney, search parties failing to locate it afterwards. "Delight thyself in the Lord, and He shall give thee the desires of thine heart."[1]

"Thou wilt shew me the path of life: in Thy presence

[1] Psalm 37, 4.

is fulness of joy: at Thy right hand are pleasures for evermore."[1]

Shall we starve in the midst of plenty?

But perhaps the unkindness of friends whom we trusted has somewhat embittered us, has robbed of our joy. The secret of His presence is comfort for us as well. "Thou shalt hide them in the secret of Thy presence from the pride of man: Thou shalt keep them secretly in a pavilion from the strife of tongues."[2] We often sing:

> O safe to the Rock that is higher than I
>> My soul mid its conflicts and sorrows would fly;
> So sinful, so weary, Thine, Thine would I be;
>> Thou blest Rock of Ages, I'm hiding in Thee.
>
> Hiding in Thee, Hiding in Thee,
>> Thou blest Rock of Ages, I'm hiding in Thee.

What is the good of singing it if we do not experience it? There is *safety* from all man's provocations in His presence.

We find in His presence *thanksgiving* and *singing*. We find in His presence *power* for every task. "The hills melted like wax at the presence, at the presence of the Lord of the whole earth."[3] Sinai was moved at the presence of the Lord.

If then, we find in His presence glory, honour, strength, gladness, joy, safety, power—shall we not consider it a privilege to be called to the Royal presence. "One thing have I desired of the Lord, that will I seek after; that I might dwell in the house of the Lord all

[1] Psalm 16, 11.   [2] Psalm 31, 20.   [3] Psalm 97, 5.

the days of my life, to behold the beauty of the Lord, and to inquire in His temple."[1] But this is far from the case with the majority of Christians. They live without the presence.

When we begin to study the reasons why so many believers are prevented from enjoying the presence of the Lord, we are rebuked.

It is impossible for the author to forget certain remarks made by a Belfast speaker in the Consecration meeting of the Cregagh Christian Endeavour Society. The subject was "Prayer" and in giving sundry exhortations, the speaker said:

"Make sure that you feel conscious of the presence of the Lord before you begin to pray."

The advice, I found, was not so simple as it appeared to be. I tried to put it into practice, but experienced defeat time and time again. Why? It was because I discovered a definite obstacle to this "practice of the presence." As soon as I sought to realise God's presence, the searing, searching finger of conscience began to disturb my mind. "What about such-and-such an unconfessed sin? What about this bad habit? What about that bit of deceit?" And there was no realisation of God's presence.

"If I regard iniquity in my heart, the Lord will not hear me."

It is impossible to take sin into God's presence.

Let us examine the details of obstacles which have robbed men of the joy of the presence of the Lord.

[1] Psalm 27, 4.

It was *disobedience* that proved the undoing of our first parents in Eden. "Adam and his wife hid themselves from the presence of the Lord God."

It was murderous *hatred* that led to Cain's forfeiture of the blessing. So "Cain went out from the presence of the Lord. . . ."

It was *uncleanness* which God told Moses would cause His servants to be set off from His presence. "Be ye clean, ye that bear the vessels of the Lord." We cannot serve God and be unclean before Him.

Sin is always the hindrance, the obstacle to the enjoyment of God's Holy presence. We cannot hold on to both. I know of many instances of such in the lives of Christians. The other day I received a very touching letter:

"—but somehow I began to drift. Outwardly I am making a good show of Christianity, am thought to be a good Christian, preach when opportunity arises. I have still the assurance of salvation, but am most miserable.

"What am I to do? I have got myself into trouble through pilfering. But I have lied my way out of the difficulties, but I am lost in a fog of sin. I am afraid. I am miserable."

Another young man told me: "I cannot even pray, for I have become a slave to my secret bad habits. I haven't realised God's presence for a long, long time."

And a young lady told me: "I have consciously disobeyed God in a private matter. I know what He wanted me to do, but I chose the thing that *I* wanted to do—something perfectly innocent, but not God's will. Oh, I am so unhappy. I have lost my joy. God doesn't seem to listen to me when I pray. . . ."

My own experience tallies. The most miserable months of my Christian experience were when I disobeyed, consciously and deliberately disobeyed God in a private matter. The other most miserable time of spiritual poverty was when I gave way to besetting sin. How did it feel? The heavens appeared to be as brass, and I felt a loneliness that the pleasures of sin could not drive away. I was shut out from the presence of God.

Jonah, the servant of God, rose up to flee from the presence of the Lord. He became very conscious of his loneliness. "For the men knew that he had fled from the presence of the Lord, *because he had told them.*"

Then Jonah prayed. What a pathetic prayer. "I cried by reason of my affliction unto the Lord, and *He heard me;* out of the belly of hell, cried I, and *Thou heardest my voice.*"

Many a despairing Christian has cried unto the Lord in the same way. "O cast me not from Thy presence." With penitence comes forgiveness, and the sense of the presence of God soothes the wounded soul like the balm of Gilead. David's prayer followed a confession "Against Thee, Thee only have I sinned. . . ." If we are to enjoy the wonder of fellowship and communion restored, all known sin must be confessed, otherwise it is impossible to realise the presence of God.

But the loneliness of separation from God makes us

yearn for His presence. The Psalmist asks the question "Whither shall I flee from Thy presence?" Wherever we may hide ourselves, still the thought of God's presence pursues us.

" O Lord, thou hast searched me, and known me.
Thou knowest my downsitting and mine uprising, thou understandest my thought afar off.
Thou compassest my path and my lying down, and art acquainted with all my ways.
For there is not a word in my tongue, but, lo, O Lord, thou knowest it altogether.
Thou hast beset me behind and before, and laid thine hand upon me.
Such knowledge is too wonderful for me; it is high, I cannot attain unto it.
Whither shall I go from thy spirit? or whither shall I flee from thy presence?
If I ascend up into heaven, thou art there; if I make my bed in hell, behold, thou art there.
If I take the wings of the morning, and dwell in the uttermost parts of the sea;
Even there shall thy hand lead me, and thy right hand shall hold me. . . .
Search me, O God, and know my heart: try me, and know my thoughts:
And see if there be any wicked way in me, and lead me in the way everlasting."

Psalm 139. *verses* 1-10. 23. 24.

And when at last, we realise the Divine presence, we are changed by the Lord from disobedient to obedient servants.

When Isaiah the prophet was presumably in his late 'teens, he had that wonderful vision of the presence of God. Chapter VI of his prophecy launches into the glorious theme, "I saw the Lord." What was the most impressive thing in the vision? Undoubtedly it was the revelation of the *holiness* of God the Lord. It can be truly said that young Isaiah realised as never before what it meant to be in the presence of a holy God.

"Holy, holy, holy, is the Lord of hosts: and His glory fills the whole earth."

And did this realisation of the presence mean blessing for Isaiah? It surely did. First came the thought of his own shabbiness, revealed by the perfect glory of God's majesty: the thought of his own uncleanness revealed by the perfect holiness of the presence of the Lord of Lords. It wrung from his lips the confession, "Woe is me, for I am undone; because I am a man of unclean lips, and I dwell in the midst of a people of unclean lips: for mine eyes have seen the King, the Lord of hosts."

After confession came cleansing—"thine iniquity is taken away, and thy sin purged."

But surely the most significant part of the story is found in the words that follow.

"Also I heard the voice of the Lord, saying, Whom shall I send and who will go for us? Then said I, Here am I; send me. And He said, Go—"

For Isaiah, the presence of the Lord meant *challenge, confession, cleansing, call, commission.* Was not that a personal revival? Was not that a time of refreshing from the presence of the Lord?

And what was true of Isaiah the prophet was true of many other Old Covenant and New Covenant saints— Moses, Gideon, Samuel, Saul of Tarsus. . . . And what was true of them is true of every individual.

The call to life service always originates in a personal contact, God's revelation of Himself. Some folks see visions; some folks receive the call through reading the Word; but it will be agreed that all receive the call through meeting with God on the road to some other Damascus. The Lord Jesus Christ is God's revelation of Himself to all humanity. Seek Him. It will not be hard to find Him.

Revival—individual or widespread—comes from the *presence* of the Lord. Do you seek revival? Seek the presence of the Lord. In His presence you will find the times of refreshing that you need.

The last reference to be quoted is a most important one. Let us pray for revival, individual and widespread. How shall we pray? The opening verse of Isaiah 64 is recorded by the Spirit for us.

"Oh! that Thou wouldest *rend the heavens*, that Thou wouldest come down, that the mountains might flow *at Thy presence*."

Rend the heavens.

CHAPTER XII

TIMES OF REFRESHING

TIMES of refreshing originate in the presence of the Lord. We all desire to see His presence manifested, and we know that God is quite willing to visit us in the power of His own presence. When that time comes there will be a revival—a revival which will magnify the name of Christ Jesus our Lord.

In Ottawa I felt inspired to write a prayer for the times of refreshing that we need. I give it with an appropriate tune on the next page as my closing word.

6.6.6.6.

Austrian Melody.
Harmonised by J. T. Cooper.

Lord God, the heavens rend,
    Come down and set us free:
A great revival send—
    Begin the work in me.

Remove the veil of sin
    That separates from Thee:
Lord, search our hearts within—
    Begin the work in me.

The cleansing Blood we plead;
    We claim the victory:
Thou canst supply our need—
    Begin the work in me.

Our humble prayer attend,
    Revival comes from Thee,
O Holy Ghost descend—
    Begin the work in me.

www.ingramcontent.com/pod-product-compliance
Lightning Source LLC
Chambersburg PA
CBHW071825090426
42737CB00012B/2185